Current
CONTROVERSIES

Drones

Other Books in the Current Controversies Series

Drones

Tamara Thompson, Book Editor

GREENHAVEN PRESS
A part of Gale, Cengage Learning

 GALE
CENGAGE Learning·

Farmington Hills, Mich • San Francisco • New York • Waterville, Maine
Meriden, Conn • Mason, Ohio • Chicago

GALE
CENGAGE Learning™

Judy Galens, *Manager, Frontlist Acquisitions*

LIBRARY OF CONGRESS CATALOGING-IN-PUBLICATION DATA

Drones / Tamara Thompson, book editor.
   pages cm. -- (Current controversies)
  Includes bibliographical references and index.
  ISBN 978-0-7377-7422-1 (hardcover) -- ISBN 978-0-7377-7423-8 (pbk.)
  1. Drone aircraft--United States. 2. Drone aircraft--Moral and ethical aspects--United States. 3. Drone aircraft--Government policy--United States. I. Thompson, Tamara.
  UG1242.D7D755 2015
  358.4'183--dc23
                   2015026925

Printed in the United States of America
1 2 3 4 5   20 19 18 17 16

Contents

Chapter 1: Why Are Drones Controversial?

Chapter 2: Should the Military Be Allowed to Use Drones?

Yes: The Military Should Be Allowed to Use Drones

Because drones can monitor targeted individuals over time and establish patterns of behavior, they are more likely to correctly identify their targets and can be more selective about the time of engagement, hence reducing civilian casualties. The argument that drones kill too many innocent civilians is not supported by recent facts.

Kristin Bergtora Sandvik and Kjersti Lohne

Humanitarian drones should be considered a "war dividend"—military technology from the war on terror that is now being transferred to humanitarian purposes around the globe. While more research is needed, both governmental and nongovernmental organizations are investigating how drone technology can be used to further goals of humanitarian assistance.

No: The Military Should Not Be Allowed to Use Drones

Lauren McCauley

The use of military drones represents a "slippery slope" that could lead to a state of endless war by lowering the bar for armed conflict and creating an overly broad interpretation of the rules for authorizing military force.

Deborah Dupre

Former president Jimmy Carter says US drone strikes violate the 1948 Universal Declaration of Human Rights and the extent to which the violations have gone is "disturbing."

Matthew Spurlock

The US government's program of targeted killing via drone strikes remains shrouded in secrecy, despite President Barack Obama's promise that it would be made "more transparent to the American people and the world."

Chapter 4: Should Commercial Drone Use Be Allowed?

No: Commercial Drone Use Should Not Be Allowed

Michael McCaul

In a post-9/11 world, allowing individuals to freely fly unmanned drones presents a significant threat to national security. The Department of Homeland Security must take immediate action to address drone use by civilians.

Patrick Hruby

It is frighteningly simple to turn a hobby drone into one that can cause harm. Armed drones in the hands of private citizens are inevitable, and this serious issue must be considered when establishing drone regulations.

Arthur Holland Michel

Drones present so many important challenges for privacy, safety, and civil liberties that their regulation must be thorough and thoughtful, not rushed or reactionary.

Foreword

By definition, controversies are "discussions of questions in which opposing opinions clash" (*Webster's Twentieth Century Dictionary Unabridged*). Few would deny that controversies are a pervasive part of the human condition and exist on virtually every level of human enterprise. Controversies transpire between individuals and among groups, within nations and between nations. Controversies supply the grist necessary for progress by providing challenges and challengers to the status quo. They also create atmospheres where strife and warfare can flourish. A world without controversies would be a peaceful world; but it also would be, by and large, static and prosaic.

The Series' Purpose

The purpose of the Current Controversies series is to explore many of the social, political, and economic controversies dominating the national and international scenes today. Titles selected for inclusion in the series are highly focused and specific. For example, from the larger category of criminal justice, Current Controversies deals with specific topics such as police brutality, gun control, white collar crime, and others. The debates in Current Controversies also are presented in a useful, timeless fashion. Articles and book excerpts included in each title are selected if they contribute valuable, long-range ideas to the overall debate. And wherever possible, current information is enhanced with historical documents and other relevant materials. Thus, while individual titles are current in focus, every effort is made to ensure that they will not become quickly outdated. Books in the Current Controversies series will remain important resources for librarians, teachers, and students for many years.

In addition to keeping the titles focused and specific, great care is taken in the editorial format of each book in the series. Book introductions and chapter prefaces are offered to provide background material for readers. Chapters are organized around several key questions that are answered with diverse opinions representing all points on the political spectrum. Materials in each chapter include opinions in which authors clearly disagree as well as alternative opinions in which authors may agree on a broader issue but disagree on the possible solutions. In this way, the content of each volume in Current Controversies mirrors the mosaic of opinions encountered in society. Readers will quickly realize that there are many viable answers to these complex issues. By questioning each author's conclusions, students and casual readers can begin to develop the critical thinking skills so important to evaluating opinionated material.

Current Controversies is also ideal for controlled research. Each anthology in the series is composed of primary sources taken from a wide gamut of informational categories including periodicals, newspapers, books, US and foreign government documents, and the publications of private and public organizations. Readers will find factual support for reports, debates, and research papers covering all areas of important issues. In addition, an annotated table of contents, an index, a book and periodical bibliography, and a list of organizations to contact are included in each book to expedite further research.

Perhaps more than ever before in history, people are confronted with diverse and contradictory information. During the Persian Gulf War, for example, the public was not only treated to minute-to-minute coverage of the war, it was also inundated with critiques of the coverage and countless analyses of the factors motivating US involvement. Being able to sort through the plethora of opinions accompanying today's major issues, and to draw one's own conclusions, can be a complicated and frustrating struggle. It is the editors' hope that Current Controversies will help readers with this struggle.

Introduction

> *"There are as many potential uses for drones as there are types of them, so whether drone technology should be considered a positive thing or a dangerous thing depends very much on who one asks."*

Even when technology has the power to dramatically reshape the world—like atomic energy or the Internet—it is still frequently regarded as being neutral, meaning the technology itself is considered neither inherently good nor bad and its impact depends entirely on how it is used.

Such is certainly the case for drones, a catch-all term that represents a wide array of remotely controlled, unmanned aerial vehicles—typically outfitted with cameras—that range greatly in shape and size. Some drones are as small as an insect or shaped like a flying saucer, while others are as big as a standard airplane and look like one as well.

There are as many potential uses for drones as there are types of them, so whether drone technology should be considered a positive thing or a dangerous thing depends very much on who one asks. Each type of drone use comes with its own set of potential benefits and problems, and as with other emerging technologies, unforeseen consequences may reveal themselves as the technology is further developed and more widely adopted.

To the military, drones are an important modern weapon that allows the United States to conduct essential surveillance and carry out targeted killings of terrorists in faraway lands without risking the lives of US service members. The military credits the US drone strike program with eliminating thousands of suspected Islamic militants and believes drones are a vital element of national security that could one day replace manned aircraft entirely.

To human rights advocates and antiwar activists, however, military drones are killing machines that indiscriminately terrorize indigenous communities and kill people who present little or no risk to the United States, including countless civilians. The ease and anonymity of using drones, they say, allows the military to take lives without the due process of law or a congressional declaration of war and without sufficient transparency, accountability, or oversight.

To domestic law enforcement agencies, drones are a new and powerful tool for finding missing persons in rugged terrain, providing aerial views of hostage standoffs, tracking fleeing crime suspects, and searching for survivors following natural disasters. Drones are especially attractive to law enforcement because they cost a fraction of what helicopters or planes cost to operate and they keep officers out of harm's way.

To many Americans, however, the use of drones by police raises serious questions about their potential for invasions of privacy, illegal searches, mass surveillance, and even weaponization. Critics fear law-enforcement drones will eventually be used to conduct routine warrantless surveillance, monitor lawful activity, and be used to troll for evidence of crimes in incidental video and images gathered during drone flights for other purposes.

Public backlash on the issue prompted the Seattle Police Department to abandon its nascent drone program in 2013—one of the few selectively permitted by the Federal Aviation Administration (FAA)—and many state and local governments have preemptively banned or significantly restricted the use of law-enforcement drones since then.

Similarly, the use of military-style spy drones by the US Customs and Border Protection agency to conduct surveillance for illegal immigration, drug smuggling, and border security has generated backlash about their potential use and misuse against American citizens, to the extent that some states and local governments have enacted laws banning government drones in their airspace.

That such strong negative sentiment has taken hold even before drones have been widely adopted by American law enforcement—indeed, even before the FAA has enacted guidelines for their use—is quite telling of the mixed feelings Americans have about drone technology. Because while the public is clearly wary of drones in the hands of law enforcement and government entities, consumers are going crazy for small, inexpensive hobby drones, and interest in using them for commercial purposes is massive.

To consumers, cheap and easy-to-fly quadcopter drones are a popular and fun way to shoot photos or video and play with technology, so much so that in 2015 global sales of consumer drones hit 4.3 million units worth about $1.7 billion—a 167 percent sales spike in just two years. But those same hobby drones can be put to endless commercial uses, which have traditionally been prohibited by the FAA.

The market for commercial drones is poised to explode, however, pending the expected September 2015 enactment of new FAA regulations that for the first time specify how and when commercial drones may be used. The FAA estimates that one hundred thousand commercial drones could take to the skies by 2017 under its new rules, which won't be broad enough to allow for the delivery of goods in most cases. (See chapter 4 for more on commercial drone use.) The FAA's regulations can't come a moment too soon for many.

To businesses, industries, and entrepreneurs nationwide, drones represent a giant leap forward in efficiency, economy, and ability. The Hollywood film industry has been clamoring to use drones for years, as have commercial photographers of all stripes. Journalists want them for live traffic reports and other newsgathering tasks, while real estate agents are eager to give their clients a drone-eye-view of listed properties. Fire departments are eyeing drones to map wildfires, monitor the position of fire crews, and assess the safety of burning buildings. Wildlife groups favor drones to prevent poaching and count animals, and the agriculture industry wants drones to keep an eye on crops and livestock and to monitor water and soil conditions. Topographical mapping, geographic surveys, and oil and gas exploration are just a few of the many other important roles that drones are expected to play in this new growth industry that will soon become an economic powerhouse. The Association for Unmanned Vehicle Systems International (AUVSI), a pro-drone industry group, estimates that drones will create more than one hundred thousand new jobs by 2025 and generate some $82.1 billion in economic benefit between 2015 and 2025.[1]

To others, though, a sky filled with drones means a sky filled with risk and danger.

When drones malfunction and fall, they can badly injure people, and drone operators can make dangerous piloting mistakes that jeopardize safety as well. There have already been cases of athletes being hit by drones filming their sporting events, drones crashing into buildings, and a variety of other incidents in which individuals' hair or hands got caught in drone rotors. Of special concern is that, despite being prohibited near airports, hobby drones have already been involved in dozens of documented near misses with commercial aircraft, a potentially deadly interaction.

To sexual predators and other criminals, drones are an easy way to watch children, case houses, peep in windows, deal drugs, and keep lookout for the police during a crime. Officials also worry that consumer drones could be turned

1. Darryl Jenkins and Bijan Vasigh, "The Economic Impact of Unmanned Aircraft Systems Integration in the United States," Association for Unmanned Vehicle Systems International, March 2013. https://higherlogicdownload.s3.amazonaws.com/AUVSI /958c920a-7f9b-4ad2-9807-f9a4e95d1ef1/UploadedImages/New_Economic%20Report %202013%20Full.pdf.

into weapons or that terrorists could use them to gather intelligence and deliver explosives to targets within the United States.

Nevertheless, with the demand for domestic drones so strong and the FAA set to release rules for their operation, their widespread use is all but inevitable for law enforcement, government agencies, commercial enterprises, and consumers alike. Regardless of how drones are ultimately used, they clearly represent a revolutionary technology that is destined to reshape the world.

The authors in *Current Controversies: Drones* present a wide variety of viewpoints about the promises and perils of drones and explore the questions of whether their use by law enforcement, consumers, businesses, and the military should be permitted.

CHAPTER 1

Why Are Drones Controversial?

Overview: Do Drones Promise Protection or Peril?

Margaret Steen

Margaret Steen is a contributing writer for Emergency Management *magazine.*

Imagine giving firefighters the ability to identify hot spots in a wildfire, through real-time images, without risking the lives of staff members—or helping search and rescue teams scan a large area quickly for survivors after a disaster.

The technology to do this exists and is being used by some public safety agencies already with unmanned aerial vehicles. But UAVs (unmanned aerial vehicles) have drawbacks, as well. Some agencies are adopting them, but concerns about safety, regulation and privacy are slowing the process.

UAVs are the vehicles flown by unmanned aircraft systems, or UASes, which include the aircraft and all the equipment required to control it. Both terms are used by those in the field. A more common name for them, drones, is not considered accurate by those who work most closely with the technology.

"Drones were remote-controlled aircraft that were targets for missiles," said Todd Sedlak, director of sales and flight operations and small UAS subject matter expert for Detroit Aircraft. The public sees them as "a mindless thing that does one thing." He said UAVs have the capacity "to save lives, to help people and to prevent damage to equipment, property and people."

UAVs come in all sizes: Some fit in the palm of a hand, while others are as large as full-size aircraft. There are two

Margaret Steen, "Are Unmanned Aircraft a Savior or Threat?," *Emergency Management*, November 12, 2014. Emergencymgmt.com.

main types of UAVs: fixed-wing, which resemble airplanes and need runways, and vertical takeoff and landing, which can hover.

The U.S. Forest Service has been exploring potential uses of UAVs and UASes for several years, said Jennifer Jones, public affairs specialist with the agency's Washington office.

UAVs could help monitor the condition of forests, determine the effectiveness of reforestation efforts or assess damage from events such as fires, landslides or floods.

"We're very interested in this technology, and we've identified a lot of potential missions they could be used for," Jones said. "And we have used them in a few cases very successfully."

Some Examples of Use

The Forest Service used unmanned aircraft in a partnership with the California Air National Guard to fight the 2013 Rim Fire. In the response to the fire, the UAVs allowed the incident team "to view events while they were happening," said Jones. The equipment was used, for example, to verify new hot spots and detect the perimeter of the fire.

"It provided live, real-time images that could supplement those traditional nighttime infrared flights," Jones said.

The Forest Service's mission extends beyond fighting fires. There are several other ways UAVs could be used:

- Forest protection and management: UAVs could help monitor the condition of forests, determine the effectiveness of reforestation efforts or assess damage from events such as fires, landslides or floods. They could also help detect and map damage from insects, diseases and invasive plant species.

- Watershed management: UAVs could monitor the condition and boundaries of watersheds and sample air quality at various altitudes.

- Fish, wildlife and plant management: UAVs could help map habitats and survey fish and wildlife populations. They could also monitor the populations of threatened and endangered fish, wildlife and plant species.

- Law enforcement: Authorities could use UAVs to help detect activities like narcotics production and timber theft.

- Post-fire response: UAVs could help map burn severity, evaluate debris flow and monitor vegetation recovery and ongoing flooding threats to downstream communities.

The Forest Service does not have a formal program in place for using UAVs, but it does have a working group looking at how it could use the systems. There could be advantages in terms of cost, safety and flying in locations and under conditions where manned aircraft couldn't be used.

An aircraft will search every square inch that you tell it to. . . . It will never get tired; it will never get bored.

The Forest Service is not the only agency that's moving slowly on the use of UAVs. The California Department of Forestry and Fire Protection (Cal Fire) has tested them in partnership with other agencies to see if they give commanders better real-time information about fires. But Cal Fire has no plans to use unmanned aircraft regularly, though it continues to evaluate them. "We're constantly looking at new technology," said Lynne Tolmachoff, a spokesperson for Cal Fire.

One agency that has been using UAVs for several years is the Mesa County Sheriff's Office in Colorado. The program has flown more than 55 missions, totaling more than 225 flight hours.

A Multitude of Uses

Unmanned aerial vehicles (UAVs) have a number of potential uses for emergency response and public safety:

Search and rescue A UAV "can search a very large area very accurately and quickly," said Todd Sedlak, director of sales and flight operations and small UAS subject matter expert for Detroit Aircraft. This can be particularly helpful for water rescue, since a warm body in cold water shows up quickly on thermal cameras. In the mountains after an avalanche, a UAV can search in conditions where it's too dangerous to send a manned aircraft. "An aircraft will search every square inch that you tell it to," he said. "It will never get tired; it will never get bored."

Situational awareness for first responders "Let's say a SWAT team has to serve a high-risk warrant—they have the ability to have a good view of the neighborhood, and if a suspect were to flee, where they're going," Sedlak said.

Traffic control UAVs can help authorities see where traffic is backing up during a major event like a football game, or to get an aerial view of the aftermath of a traffic accident. A UAV is "a low-cost, safe and easy-to-use alternative to anything that police are already using helicopters for," Sedlak said.

There are several uncertainties and concerns regarding [UAV] use, and these have slowed some agencies' efforts.

Firefighting A UAV with a thermal camera can show whether the roof of a building has fire underneath it—a faster and safer way to make this determination than having a firefighter climb on the roof and use a hammer to find soft spots. It also can help determine what other buildings are at risk based on the wind speed and direction. In a forest fire, a

UAV's camera can see through the forest canopy to show where fire is spreading below. "This is already being done with manned aircraft," said Sedlak. "This is cheaper, faster and safer."

A Cost-Effective Answer

The sheriff's office first acquired an unmanned helicopter in 2009 and worked with the FAA to get a certificate of authorization that would allow the department to fly it. By the fall of 2010, the sheriff's office had FAA permission to use the system anywhere in the county during the day, and it expanded its tests and started using the UAV to help other agencies with aerial photos during the response to events like fires and fatal traffic accidents.

In 2012, the department tested a fixed-wing UAV, which has a longer flight time than the helicopter and could be used for more searches or fire monitoring over larger areas. Now the department is beginning to use the systems for day-to-day operations.

One of the advantages UAVs offer public safety and emergency management officials is that they can see areas that are otherwise inaccessible because of the danger to human pilots. Another big advantage is cost.

Mesa County officials estimate that the UAVs they use would cost between $25,000 and $50,000 each. (They have spent much less because they have partnerships with the manufacturers to help test the systems.) Larger systems would cost even more.

However, the costs are still much less than for flying manned aircraft. Mesa County officials project that the long-term operating costs of their UAVs is about $25 per hour. Planes and helicopters with pilots can cost between $400 and $1,200 per hour to operate.

Safety in the Spotlight

If UAVs provide such great help to public safety agencies at such a low cost, why aren't they being more quickly adopted? There are several uncertainties and concerns regarding their use, and these have slowed some agencies' efforts.

One issue is safety. UAVs are considered aircraft, and some can be quite large. This is one issue that the Forest Service's advisory group is looking at, Jones said. "Our top priority in the Forest Service is safety," she said. That includes the safety of firefighters and other agency employees, as well as the safety of the public.

"They can pose a risk to people on the ground if one of those is flying overhead and a communications link is lost," said Jones. "We've got to make sure that we can fly them safely, given the other aircraft that are often flying in fire environments."

There are other details to be worked out, as well, Jones said. "We're trying to define the mission requirements." A lot of missions can also be performed by manned aircraft, and the agency wants to determine when officials would turn to UAVs and who would operate them.

There's also some uncertainty about how UAVs will ultimately be regulated. Private citizens can buy and operate their own UAVs as a hobby, with few restrictions from the FAA as long as they are not flown too high or too close to an airport. The FAA hasn't issued specific regulations about when UAVs can be used by people who are being paid to operate them, however. The FAA is working on rules that would allow commercial use of certain UAVs in some circumstances.

Public agencies are able to get a certificate of authorization from the FAA to use unmanned aircraft under certain circumstances. But these can take a long time to receive, so most agencies can't simply buy a UAV and start using it.

Privacy Concerns

Another big concern is privacy. The Seattle Police Department last year [2013] abandoned a program to use UAVs while it was still in the planning and testing phase because of public concerns about privacy. It ended up giving the UAVs to the Los Angeles Police Department, which has said it won't use them until the city decides on terms for their implementation into operations.

A number of states have passed or are considering laws that would limit the ways law enforcement could use UAVs, such as requiring a warrant for many uses.

A final hurdle for some agencies is the rapid development of the technology, which can make decisions difficult.

Although UAVs may be sent to photograph wildfires and storms in situations where sending a manned aircraft is too dangerous, in urban settings most of what they are documenting could also be photographed by manned aircraft. The concerns raised by privacy advocates stem from their low cost and ease of use: If UAVs can be operated cheaply and easily, what is to prevent law enforcement from conducting constant surveillance?

"Commonsense Checks and Balances"

"Our main concern is the suspicion-less use for mass surveillance," said Jay Stanley, a privacy expert with the Speech, Privacy and Technology Program of the American Civil Liberties Union [ACLU]. He said the ACLU is not opposed to all uses of UAVs. "I don't think anybody objects to the use of a drone to find a lost child in the woods. Or if the police are raiding a crime kingpin's home and want some aerial support and have a warrant to raid the home, we wouldn't object to that. We just want to put in place some commonsense checks and balances."

There are also questions about what secondary uses of the video are acceptable, Stanley said. For example, what if authorities collect video of a large area to assess damage after an earthquake but later decide to examine the footage to look for evidence of people growing marijuana? That could provide evidence that in other situations they would have needed a warrant to collect.

A final hurdle for some agencies is the rapid development of the technology, which can make decisions difficult.

"Every year something new and better is coming out," said Tolmachoff of Cal Fire. "We're looking at all avenues. We're still researching and trying to figure out which one will work best for our department."

Military Use Gives Peaceful Drones a Bad Reputation

Ben Acheson

Ben Acheson is a policy adviser at the European Parliament in Brussels, Belgium.

D rones kill innocent civilians. What else is there to say?

This is the go-to argument for many opponents of 're-motely piloted air systems' (RPAS) or unmanned aerial ve-hicles (UAVs). Even when drones eliminate 'legitimate' targets, their use sparks fervent public outrage. The recent media frenzy over the killing of [Islamic militant] Hakimullah Meh-sud confirmed as much.

Mehsud's four-year reign as head of Pakistan's most bar-baric militant group was characterised by brutal attacks on soldiers, government officials and civilians, but his death still caused widespread consternation. The government of Pakistan described the attack as a "violation of Pakistan's sovereignty and territorial integrity" and bemoaned that it derailed efforts at peaceful dialogue. Predictably, eristic peace activists relished the media coverage as a platform to condemn US forces.

Even before Mehsud's death, a UN human rights investiga-tor called for a moratorium on the testing and use of 'lethal autonomous robots' due to the lack of legal accountability. The 'War Child' charity echoed concerns and suggested that drones will lead to increased child casualties in future wars.

So if we condemn drone attacks when they don't get the bad guys, but we also denounce them when they do, should we just ban the technology altogether?

No. The public debate on drones is too focused on targeted killings. The very mention of the word 'drone' conjures images of Islamic militants scarpering across a dusty desert whilst unmanned, emotionless killing machines whirl ominously in the skies above. Consequently, the use of drones in more peaceful settings, such as agricultural pest control and high resolution imagery, is routinely overlooked.

Drone Debate Demands Reason, Not Reaction

To brand the entire technology as 'immoral' is unfair. The drone debate must be approached with reason, not hijacked by the same type of short-sighted, hysterical activists whose blind, misguided ideology focuses more on banning every type of human development which, with refinements, could actually aid some of their own overarching aims.

Many drones are designed purely to save lives, rather than take them.

Most people partner drones with the 'War on Terror' in Afghanistan, Pakistan and Yemen, but the technology actually dates back to 1917 when the Hewitt-Sperry Automatic Airplane made its maiden flight in the United States. The first armed drones were not used until the Iran-Iraq war in the 1980s.

Two decades later, the US employed weaponised drones in Pakistan's tribal areas. Since 2004, nearly 400 strikes have hit the region, killing many al-Qaeda leaders and Taliban militants. However, civilian fatalities have overshadowed the efficacy of these strikes because groups of men are often targeted based on behaviour patterns rather than known identities.

The backlash is not wholly unwarranted. Around 2,200 people have been killed and at least 400 of those were civilians. A recent UN investigation identified 33 drone strikes that resulted in civilian casualties and violated international humanitarian law. The criticism has mainly been levied at the US due to its reluctance to declassify information about CIA operations. A senior UN official even commented that the CIA's intransigence caused "an almost insurmountable obstacle to transparency".

Some Drones Save Lives

The oft-overlooked fact is that the military is not the only user of remotely piloted aircraft. Many drones are designed purely to save lives, rather than take them. RPAS technology helps air traffic controllers and those who create high resolution imagery. It is also being developed in conjunction with science, agriculture, environmental protection, transport and border security.

Drones are already used for whale spotting, academic research, rescue missions, sports and filming. They help prevent elephants from trampling on crops and deter poachers in Kenya. The 'Defikopter' is a defibrillator-carrying drone which can be on-hand to administer first aid within minutes. It can fly up to 43 miles an hour and isn't affected by a paramedic's worst enemy—traffic.

In the future, drones will fight forest fires. There are also plans to use unmanned drones to battle mosquitos. The insects are becoming such a problem in Florida that Florida Keys Mosquito Control is using drones with shortwave infrared cameras to locate pools where larvae are most likely being hatched.

Even Domino's is getting in on the action. The pizza-making giant is testing delivery by Domicopter; a robotic remote-controlled helicopter. This is surely nothing more than a clever marketing ploy, but it is not unprecedented. GPS-operated drones have also been used to deliver beer to revellers at the South African OppiKoppi music festival.

Moving the Conversation Forward

Pizza and beer aside, the legal moral, ethical and human rights implications of the targeted killing programmes undoubtedly deserve the highest levels of attention, but the drone debate needs to move beyond the confines of the current discussion.

Drones are not just emotionless killing machines. Yes, some targeted killings go wrong. Yes, civilian casualties are *intolerable*. Yet it is up to the law of armed conflict to set limits on the military use of RPAS and provide guidance on military necessity, proportionality, surrender and the treatment of combatants.

Drone technology is ultimately a useful tool. It brings a competitive advantage to the battlefield. It will continue to be used by the military. We must not forget that UAVs may alter how some military tasks are conducted but they do not change what the military must accomplish. Beyond the battlefield, drones will soon assume a more prominent, and important, role in peaceful activities.

Campaigning for a ban on the technology is not only disproportionate; it is ridiculous. The inarguable fact is that, whether we like it or not, drone technology is the future.

No-Fly Zone: How "Drone" Safety Rules Can Also Help Protect Privacy

John Villasenor

John Villasenor is a nonresident senior fellow in governance studies at the Center for Technology Innovation at the Brookings Institution.

For most of the 20th century, obtaining overhead images was difficult and expensive. Now, thanks to advances in unmanned aircraft systems (UAS)—people in the aviation field tend to dislike the word *drone*—it has become easy and inexpensive, raising new and important privacy issues. These issues need to be addressed primarily through legal frameworks: The Constitution, existing and new federal and state laws, and legal precedents regarding invasion of privacy will all play key roles in determining the bounds of acceptable information-gathering from UAS. But safety regulations will have an important and less widely appreciated secondary privacy role.

Why? Because safety regulations, which aim to ensure that aircraft do not pose a danger in the airspace or to people and property on the ground, obviously place restrictions on where and in what manner aircraft can be operated. Those same restrictions can also affect privacy from overhead observations from both government and nongovernment UAS. FAA [Federal Aviation Administration] regulations make it unlawful, for example, to operate any aircraft (whether manned or unmanned) "in a careless or reckless manner so as to endanger the life or property of another." Aircraft must also be operated at a sufficiently high altitude to allow "an emergency landing without undue hazard to persons or property on the surface" in the event of an engine failure. Flying a UAS around someone else's backyard can be a bad idea for lots of reasons, including the possibility of violating these rules.

"Line of Sight" Rules

UAS safety (and other) regulations are in the midst of an overhaul. Last year [2012], President [Barack] Obama signed an FAA reauthorization bill that provides for the integration of UAS into the national airspace by late 2015. Under this new law, since May 2012 law enforcement agencies have been able to apply for expedited authorizations to use certain types of small UAS, which must be operated during daylight, less than 400 feet above the ground, and within "line of sight" of the operator. This means that the operator can see a UAS with his or her own eyes as it is being flown. (The phrase "visual line of sight" is sometimes distinguished from "line of sight," which can refer to operation in which a radio signal can be transmitted directly from an operator to a UAS that may be beyond visual line of sight. However, in the 2012 FAA reauthorization bill, "line of sight" is almost certainly intended to mean "visual line of sight.")

An individual, company, or other organization that runs afoul of FAA rules could face fines or other legal consequences and find its authorization to operate unmanned aircraft suspended or revoked.

Visual line of sight operation is also required under a definition provided for "model aircraft" in the 2012 law. However, that definition is specific to that section of the law and may not apply to all hobbyist unmanned aircraft. The FAA's Advisory Circular on "model aircraft operating standards" does not mention line of sight, though model aircraft operation beyond the line of sight would risk being viewed by the FAA as careless or reckless. The FAA is also very likely to require visual line of sight operation in new rules for most (but not all) commercial, research, and other uses of UAS.

FAA Rules Are Disincentive to Abuse Drones

From the FAA's standpoint, line-of-sight rules are aimed solely at ensuring safety, since an operator who can't see the aircraft he or she is flying can find it harder to "see and avoid" other aircraft in the vicinity. But line-of-sight operation also provides some measure of privacy protection by excluding some of the most egregious potential abuses. It is very hard for an operator in front of a house to maintain visual line of sight while lowering an unmanned aircraft into the fenced-in backyard to obtain eye-level images through the back windows of the house.

While there is nothing physically preventing an unmanned aircraft from being flown in violation of these and other FAA rules, the potential consequences of doing so can provide a strong set of disincentives. An individual, company, or other organization that runs afoul of FAA rules could face fines or other legal consequences and find its authorization to operate unmanned aircraft suspended or revoked. That may not stop the most determined paparazzi from snapping overhead pictures of sunbathing movie stars, but it should help dissuade many would-be UAS voyeurs.

And what would happen if a law enforcement agency violated FAA rules while using a UAS to get images of a suspect's backyard? Would acquiring those images be a Fourth Amendment "search," and therefore be unconstitutional without a warrant?

Prior Case Law

While the Supreme Court has never specifically ruled on UAS privacy, it considered warrantless observations from manned government aircraft on three occasions in the 1980s. In the 1986 *California v. Ciraolo* decision, for instance, the court ruled that police observations from an airplane flying at 1,000 feet of marijuana growing in a backyard were constitutional. Noting that the "observations . . . took place within public navigable airspace . . . in a physically nonintrusive manner," the court held that the "Fourth Amendment simply does not require the police traveling in the public airways at this altitude to obtain a warrant in order to observe what is visible to the naked eye." In two other decisions involving observations of private property from aircraft—*Dow Chemical Co. v. United States* in 1986 and *Florida v. Riley* in 1989—the justices also viewed the fact that the aircraft were lawfully operated as a factor, although far from the only one, in finding no Fourth Amendment violation. In light of these precedents, a court might well find gathering images from government aircraft operated in violation of FAA regulations to be unconstitutional.

It's still far too early to know exactly how FAA rules designed to provide safety and efficiency will affect unmanned aircraft privacy. Commercial UAS operation in the United States is not yet permitted, and the number of law enforcement organizations that have received FAA authorizations for operational (as opposed to training) UAS use is still very limited. And while there is a large and growing community of "drone" hobbyists, the overwhelming majority of them fly safely and in a manner respecting privacy.

However, as unmanned aircraft use increases there will inevitably be instances in which UAS are operated by private individuals, paparazzi, companies, and law enforcement agencies in ways that raise privacy concerns. Determining whether those uses violate reasonable expectations of privacy will sometimes start—though certainly not end—with an inquiry into whether the UAS was operated in compliance with FAA regulations.

Drone Use Takes Off Despite Safety Concerns, Restrictions

Joan Lowy

Joan Lowy is a staff writer for the Associated Press, a news wire service.

The government is getting near-daily reports—and sometimes two or three a day—of drones flying near airplanes and helicopters or close to airports without permission, federal and industry officials told The Associated Press. It's a sharp increase from just two years ago when such reports were still unusual.

Many of the reports are filed with the Federal Aviation Administration by airline pilots. But other pilots, airport officials and local authorities often file reports as well, said the officials, who agreed to discuss the matter only on the condition that they not be named because they weren't authorized to speak publicly.

Michael Toscano, president of a drone industry trade group, said FAA officials also have verified the increase to him.

While many of the reports are unconfirmed, raising the possibility that pilots may have mistaken a bird or another plane in the distance for a drone, the officials said other reports appear to be credible.

The FAA tightly restricts the use of drones, which could cause a crash if one collided with a plane or was sucked into an engine. Small drones usually aren't visible on radar to air traffic controllers, particularly if they're made of plastic or other composites.

"It should not be a matter of luck that keeps an airplane and a drone apart," said Rory Kay, a training captain at a major airline and a former Air Line Pilots Association safety committee chairman. "So far we've been lucky because if these things are operating in the sky unregulated, unmonitored and uncontrolled, the possibility of a close proximity event or even a collision has to be of huge concern."

In some cases the FAA has "identified unsafe and unauthorized (drone) operations and contacted the individual operators to educate them about how they can operate safely under current regulations and laws."

The FAA requires that all drone operators receive permission from the agency, called a certificate of authorization, before they can fly their unmanned aircraft. Most certificates limit drones to 400 feet in altitude and require that they remain within sight of the operator and at least 5 miles away from an airport. Exceptions are made for some government drones. The military flies drones in great swaths of airspace in remote areas designated for military use. Customs and Border Protection flies high-altitude drones along the U.S. borders with Mexico and Canada.

Jim Williams, who heads the FAA drone office, caused a stir earlier this year when he told a drone industry conference that an airliner nearly collided with a drone over Tallahassee, Florida, in March. The pilot of the 50-seat Canadair Regional Jet reported the camouflage-painted drone was at an altitude of about 2,300 feet, 5 miles northeast of the airport. The FAA hasn't been able to find the drone or identify its operator.

Some other recent incidents:

- The pilots of a regional airliner flying at about 10,000 feet reported seeing at least one drone pass less than 500 feet above the plane moving slowly to the south toward Allegheny County Airport near Pittsburgh. The drone was described as black and gray with a thin body, about 5 feet to 6 feet long.

- Air traffic controllers in Burbank, California, received a report from a helicopter pilot of a camera-equipped drone flying near the giant Hollywood sign.

- Controllers at central Florida's approach control facility received a report from the pilots of an Airbus A319 airliner that they had sighted a drone below the plane at about 11,000 feet and 15 miles west of Orlando. The drone was described as having a red vertical stabilizer and blue body. It wasn't picked up on radar.

- The pilots of a regional airliner reported spotting a drone 500 feet to 1,000 feet off the plane's right side during a landing approach to runway 4 of the Greenville-Spartanburg International Airport in South Carolina. The drone was described as the size of a large bird.

- A 5-foot-long drone with an attached camera crashed near Dallas Love Field in Texas. The wreckage was discovered by a worker at a factory near the airport. Police said they were looking for the operator.

In some cases the FAA has "identified unsafe and unauthorized (drone) operations and contacted the individual operators to educate them about how they can operate safely under current regulations and laws," the agency said in a statement. The FAA also said rogue operators have been threatened with fines.

Aviation safety expert John Goglia, a former National Transportation Safety Board member, said he's skeptical of some of the reports because most of the small drones currently being sold can't reach the altitudes cited by pilots. Still, "it needs to be run to ground. That means a real investigation, real work done to determine just what these reports mean," he said.

More than 1 million small drones have been sold worldwide in the past few years, said Toscano, the official with the drone industry group. It is inevitable that some will misuse them because they don't understand the safety risks or simply don't care, he said.

"This technology has a phenomenal upside that people are still just trying to understand," he said. "As unfortunate as it would be that we have an incident, it's not going to shut down the industry."

The FAA is expected to propose regulations before the end of the year that would allow broader commercial use of drones weighing less than 55 pounds. The FAA prohibits nearly all commercial use of drones, although that ban is being challenged. So far, the only commercial permits the agency has granted have been to two oil companies operating in Alaska and seven aerial photography companies associated with movie and television production.

But the ban has been ignored by many other drone operators, from real estate agents to urban planners to farmers who use them to monitor crops.

Safely Adding Drones to US Airspace Is a Formidable Challenge

US Department of Transportation Office of Inspector General

The Office of Inspector General at the US Department of Transportation (DOT) provides Congress with independent, objective reviews of the efficiency and effectiveness of DOT operations and programs and works to detect and prevent fraud, waste, and abuse.

The Federal Aviation Administration (FAA) forecasts there will be roughly 7,500 active Unmanned Aircraft Systems (UAS) in the United States in 5 years, with over $89 billion invested in UAS worldwide over the next 10 years. Unmanned aircraft range in size from those smaller than a radio-controlled model airplane to those with a wingspan as large as a Boeing 737. These aircraft can serve diverse purposes, such as enhancing border security, monitoring forest fires, and aiding law enforcement, as well as potential commercial use, such as food and package delivery. Due in part to the safety risks associated with integrating UAS into the National Airspace System (NAS), FAA authorizes UAS operations only on a limited, case-by-case basis. While the capabilities of unmanned aircraft have significantly improved, they have a limited ability to detect, sense, and avoid other air traffic.

Concerned with the progress of integrating UAS into the NAS, Congress established specific UAS provisions and deadlines for FAA in the FAA Modernization and Reform Act of 2012. These actions include publishing a 5-year roadmap, es-

US Department of Transportation, "FAA Faces Significant Barriers to Safely Integrate Unmanned Aircraft Systems into the National Airspace System," Office of Inspector General Audit Report, June 26, 2014.

tablishing six test ranges, and completing the safe integration of UAS into the NAS by September 2015. The Chairmen and Ranking Members of the Senate Commerce Committee and the House Committee on Transportation and Infrastructure, and those Committees' Aviation Subcommittees, requested that we assess FAA's progress in these efforts. Accordingly, our audit objectives were to assess (1) FAA's efforts to mitigate safety risks for integrating UAS into the NAS, and (2) FAA's progress and challenges in meeting the UAS requirements cited in the act.

While it is certain that FAA will accommodate UAS operations at limited locations, it is uncertain when and if full integration of UAS into the NAS will occur.

We conducted this review in accordance with generally accepted Government auditing standards.

FAA Faces a Variety of Barriers

Significant technological, regulatory, and management barriers exist to safely integrate UAS into the NAS. First, following many years of working with industry, FAA has not reached consensus on standards for technology that would enable UAS to detect and avoid other aircraft and ensure reliable data links between ground stations and the unmanned aircraft they control. Second, FAA has not established a regulatory framework for UAS integration, such as aircraft certification requirements, standard air traffic procedures for safely managing UAS with manned aircraft, or an adequate controller training program for managing UAS. Third, FAA is not effectively collecting and analyzing UAS safety data to identify risks. This is because FAA has not developed procedures for ensuring that all UAS safety incidents are reported and tracked or a process for sharing UAS safety data with the U.S. Department of Defense (DoD), the largest user of UAS. Finally, FAA is not effectively managing its oversight of UAS operations. Although FAA established a UAS Integration Office, it has not clarified lines of reporting or established clear guidance for UAS regional inspectors on authorizing and overseeing UAS operations. Until FAA addresses these barriers, UAS integration will continue to move at a slow pace, and safety risks will remain.

FAA's efforts to integrate UAS depend on ensuring that UAS technology is advanced and robust enough to operate safely in the same airspace as manned aircraft.

Behind Schedule

FAA is making some progress in meeting UAS-related provisions of the FAA Modernization and Reform Act of 2012, but the Agency is significantly behind schedule in meeting most of them, including the goal of achieving safe integration by September 2015. FAA has completed 9 of the act's 17 UAS provisions, such as selecting 6 test sites, publishing a UAS Roadmap, and developing a comprehensive plan outlining FAA's UAS plans in the near- and long-term. However, the Agency missed the statutory milestones for most of these provisions, and much work remains to fully implement them. FAA is also behind schedule in implementing the remaining eight UAS provisions. For example, FAA will not meet the August 2014 milestone for issuing a final rule on small UAS operations. FAA's delays are due to unresolved technological, regulatory, and privacy issues, which will prevent FAA from meeting Congress' September 30, 2015, deadline for achieving safe UAS integration. As a result, while it is certain that FAA will accommodate UAS operations at limited locations, it is uncertain when and if full integration of UAS into the NAS will occur.

We are making recommendations to enhance the effectiveness of FAA's efforts to safely integrate UAS into the NAS. . . .

Airspace Integration Has Been Stalled

Although FAA is taking steps to advance UAS operations, significant technological barriers remain, limiting FAA's progress in achieving safe integration. In addition, FAA has not yet achieved consensus on regulatory standards for integrating UAS into the NAS, including defining minimum performance and design certification standards. FAA faces further challenges because the Agency has yet to develop standardized air traffic control (ATC) procedures specific to the unique characteristics of UAS, and the Agency has not established a sufficient framework for sharing and analyzing safety data from UAS operators. Finally, organizational barriers—such as a lack of clear lines of reporting for UAS staff—are further impeding FAA's progress in integrating and overseeing UAS operations.

FAA's efforts to integrate UAS depend on ensuring that UAS technology is advanced and robust enough to operate safely in the same airspace as manned aircraft. However, two technological barriers that pose significant UAS safety risks are delaying FAA's goals. First, because there are no pilots on board, a UAS cannot comply with the "see and avoid" requirements that underpin operational safety in the NAS. However, there is currently a lack of a mature UAS technology capable of automatically detecting other aircraft operating in nearby airspace and successfully maneuvering to avoid them. Experts we interviewed stated that "detect and avoid" is the most pressing technical challenge to integration.

Second, UAS must maintain an adequate link to ground control commands to ensure that pilots never lose control of their aircraft. However, UAS still lack the adequate technology to prevent "lost link" scenarios—disruptions between the ground based operator and the aircraft—which creates significant safety challenges for both controllers and operators. . . .

No Consensus on Regulatory Standards or Training

FAA has not established a regulatory framework for integrating UAS into the NAS. This includes defining minimum performance and design certification standards and issuing rules describing when and how UAS are authorized to operate in U.S. airspace. Instead, FAA currently allows UAS operations only on a case-by-case basis, either under COA procedures with restrictions, or Special Airworthiness Certificates in the experimental or restricted category. In both cases, the applicant submits a standardized application to FAA. FAA reviews each application to ensure that the prospective operator has mitigated safety risks to an acceptable degree. However, to move beyond case-by-case authorizations, FAA will need to establish [performance and certification] standards and guidance. . . .

In addition, FAA has not resolved many other critical issues related to regulatory requirements and standards, including UAS pilot and crew qualifications, ground control stations, and command and control reliability. . . .

Currently, although FAA has authorized some UAS to operate in the NAS at select locations, such as along the Nation's borders, the Agency has not developed the procedures, training, and tools for controllers to effectively manage UAS in the same airspace as other aircraft. . . .

As the number of UAS operating in domestic airspace increases, safety risks will persist until FAA establishes performance, air traffic control, and certification standards to regulate UAS use.

Furthermore, FAA has not provided adequate automated tools for managing UAS traffic, largely because FAA's air traffic control equipment was not developed with UAS operations in mind. . . .

FAA's efforts to integrate UAS are further limited because the Agency has not obtained comprehensive data on UAS operations. Because integrating UAS into the NAS is in the early stages, any and all data regarding the safety of UAS operations are paramount to understanding and mitigating hazards that may arise. FAA routinely collects safety data from current public use UAS operators as required by the agreements with each operator. However, the Agency does not know whether it is receiving a sufficient amount of data from UAS operators because it has not established a process to ensure that operators report all incidents as required. . . .

FAA Must Step Up

FAA's primary mission remains ensuring the safety of the NAS. As such, the FAA Modernization and Reform Act's goal of integrating unmanned aircraft into the NAS by 2015 presents unique and complex safety challenges for the Agency. Now is the time, while UAS operations are currently still limited, for FAA to build critical knowledge by collecting and analyzing UAS safety data and better managing its oversight through the UAS integration office. However, as the number of UAS operating in domestic airspace increases, safety risks will persist until FAA establishes performance, air traffic control, and certification standards to regulate UAS use. Until FAA is successful in establishing these standards and adhering to a comprehensive integration plan with other public and private stakeholders, it will remain unclear when, and if, FAA can meet its goals to safely integrate UAS.

 CONTROVERSIES

CHAPTER 2

Should the Military Be Allowed to Use Drones?

Overview:
The Global Proliferation
of Military Drones

Patrick Tucker

Patrick Tucker is technology editor for Defense One, *an online publication for national security professionals and others interested in US defense issues.*

Virtually every country on Earth will be able to build or acquire drones capable of firing missiles within the next ten years. Armed aerial drones will be used for targeted killings, terrorism and the government suppression of civil unrest. What's worse, say experts, it's too late for the United States to do anything about it.

After the past decade's explosive growth, it may seem that the U.S. is the only country with missile-carrying drones. In fact, the U.S. is losing interest in further developing armed drone technology. The military plans to spend $2.4 billion on unmanned aerial vehicles, or UAVs, in 2015. That's down considerably from the $5.7 billion that the military requested in the 2013 budget. Other countries, conversely, have shown growing interest in making unmanned robot technology as deadly as possible. Only a handful of countries have armed flying drones today, including the U.S., United Kingdom, Israel, China and (possibly) Iran, Pakistan and Russia. Other countries want them, including South Africa and India. So far, 23 countries have developed or are developing armed drones, according to a recent report from the RAND organization. It's only a matter of time before the lethal technology spreads, several experts say.

"Once countries like China start exporting these, they're going to be everywhere really quickly. Within the next 10 years, every country will have these," Noel Sharkey, a robotics and artificial intelligence professor from the University of Sheffield, told *Defense One*. "There's nothing illegal about these unless you use them to attack other countries. Anything you can [legally] do with a fighter jet, you can do with a drone."

Drones Are Spreading Fast

Sam Brannen, who analyzes drones as a senior fellow at the Center for Strategic and International Studies' International Security Program, agreed with the timeline with some caveats. Within five years, he said, every country could have access to the equivalent of an armed UAV, like General Atomics' Predator, which fires Hellfire missiles. He suggested five to 10 years as a more appropriate date for the global spread of heavier, longer range "hunter-killer" aircraft, like the MQ-9 Reaper. "It's fair to say that the U.S. is leading now in the state of the art on the high end [UAVs]" such as the RQ-170.

While the U.S. may be trying to wean itself off of armed UAV technology, many more countries are quickly becoming hooked.

"Any country that has weaponized any aircraft will be able to weaponize a UAV," said Mary Cummings, Duke University professor and former Navy fighter pilot, in a note of cautious agreement. "While I agree that within 10 years weaponized drones could be part of the inventory of most countries, I think it is premature to say that they will. . . . Such endeavors are expensive [and] require larger UAVs with the payload and range capable of carrying the additional weight, which means they require substantial sophistication in terms of the ground control station."

Not every country needs to develop an armed UAV program to acquire weaponized drones within a decade. China recently announced that it would be exporting to Saudi Arabia its Wing Loong, a Predator knock-off, a development that heralds the further roboticization of conflict in the Middle East, according to Peter Singer, Brookings fellow and author of *Wired for War: The Robotics Revolution and Conflict in the 21st Century*. "You could soon have U.S. and Chinese made drones striking in the same region," he noted.

From Science Fiction to Science Fact

Singer cautions that while the U.S. may be trying to wean itself off of armed UAV technology, many more countries are quickly becoming hooked. "What was once viewed as science fiction, and abnormal, is now normal. . . . Nations in NATO that said they would never buy drones, and then said they would never use armed drones, are now saying, 'Actually, we're going to buy them.' We've seen the U.K., France, and Italy go down that pathway. The other NATO states are right behind," Singer told *Defense One*.

Virtually any country, organization or individual could employ low-tech tactics to "weaponize" drones right now. "Not everything is going to be Predator class," said Singer. "You've got a fuzzy line between cruise missiles and drones moving forward. There will be high-end expensive ones and low-end cheaper ones." The recent use of drone surveillance and even the reported deployment of booby-trapped drones by Hezbollah, Singer said, are examples of do-it-yourself killer UAVs that will permeate the skies in the decade ahead— though more likely in the skies local to their host nation and not over American cities. "Not every nation is going to be able to carry out global strikes," he said.

Weaponized Drones Are Inevitable

So, what option does that leave U.S. policy makers wanting to govern the spread of this technology? Virtually none, say experts. "You're too late," said Sharkey, matter-of-factly.

Continued indecision by the United States regarding export of this technology will not prevent the spread of these systems.

Other experts suggest that its time the U.S. embrace the inevitable and put weaponized drone technology into the hands of additional allies. The U.S. has been relatively constrained in its willingness to sell armed drones, exporting weaponized UAV technology only to the United Kingdom, according to a recent white paper, by Brannen for CSIS. In July 2013, Congress approved the sale of up to 16 MQ-Q Reaper UAVs to France, but these would be unarmed.

"If France had possessed and used armed UAVs ... when it intervened in Mali to fight the jihadist insurgency Ansar Dine—or if the United States had operated them in support or otherwise passed on its capabilities—France would have been helped considerably. Ansar Dine has no air defenses to counter such a UAV threat," note the authors of the RAND report.

In his paper, Brennan makes the same point more forcefully. "In the midst of this growing global interest, the United States has chosen to indefinitely put on hold sales of its most capable [unmanned aerial system] to many of its allies and partners, which has led these countries to seek other suppliers or to begin efforts to indigenously produce the systems," he writes. "Continued indecision by the United States regarding export of this technology will not prevent the spread of these systems."

The Missile Technology Control Regime, or MTCR, is probably the most important piece of international policy that limits the exchange of drones and is a big reason why more countries don't have weaponized drone technology. But China never signed onto it. The best way to insure that U.S. armed drones and those of our allies can operate together is to reconsider the way MTCR should apply to drones, Brannen writes.

"U.S. export is unlikely to undermine the MTCR, which faces a larger set of challenges in preventing the proliferation of ballistic and cruise missiles, as well as addressing more problematic [unmanned]-cruise missile hybrids such as so-called loitering munitions (e.g., the Israeli-made Harop)," he writes.

Is Full Autonomy Possible?

The biggest technology challenge in drone development also promises the biggest reward in terms cost savings and functionality: full autonomy. The military is interested in drones that can do more taking off, landing and shooting on their own. UAVs have limited ability to guide themselves and the development of fully autonomous drones is years away. But some recent breakthroughs are beginning to bear fruit. The experimental X-47B, a sizable drone that can fly off of aircraft carriers, "demonstrated that some discrete tasks that are considered extremely difficult when performed by humans can be mastered by machines with relative ease," Brannen notes.

Less impressed, Sharkey said the U.S. still has time to rethink its drone future. "Don't go to the next step. Don't make them fully autonomous. That will proliferate just as quickly and then you are really going to be sunk."

Others, including Singer, disagreed. "As you talk about this moving forward, the drones that are sold and used are remotely piloted to be more and more autonomous. As the technology becomes more advanced it becomes easier for people to use. To fly a Predator, you used to need to be a pilot," he said.

"The field of autonomy is going to continue to advance regardless of what happens in the military side."

Military Drones Help Keep American Troops Safe

Keith C. Burris

Keith C. Burris is editorial page editor of the Journal Inquirer *newspaper in Manchester, Connecticut.*

Drones carry smart missiles that can be used to target enemies and encampments with incredible precision and without risking the life of a U.S. pilot.

They are unmanned, programmed, and piloted remotely—almost like a video game. And their targets are intelligence targets.

That blurs spying and war.

Drones have been used in the war on terrorists by presidents George W. Bush and Barack Obama.

Some key terrorist leaders in Iraq and Afghanistan were taken out with drones.

Drones have also been used where the USA does not have troops, or, ostensibly, a war—in Pakistan and parts of Africa. And they have been used against American citizens fighting in behalf of the Taliban.

Now some members of Congress are raising questions, saying they want more accountability regarding the government's use of drones. That's not unreasonable, though there is a generous amount of disingenuousness and posturing going on here.

There should be strict oversight of the use of drones. It's just too bad only Congress, which is generally far more irresponsible and undisciplined than the executive branch, is the only branch to do it. (Occasionally the courts do get involved, but so far this has not hampered the military or the CIA [Central Intelligence Agency].)

Yes, drones are scary.

Yes, there is potential for abuse.

Yes, there are constitutional balancing questions.

Yes, Congress is entitled to ask about civilian casualties.

[Drones] have eliminated many dangerous enemies of the United States.

And yes, the Senate is entitled to advise and consent regarding the use of drones. (Again, given the modern Senate, that's a shame.)

Yes, drones also blur assassination and war.

But the bottom line on drones is:

They have eliminated many dangerous enemies of the United States. People who wanted to kill us—a lot of us. You may not like the idea of a war on terror, but there are a lot of terrorists out there, and the USA is Target No. 1.

Drones have been more successful than the conventional wars in Iran and Afghanistan. That is startlingly true. Their results have been better, with many fewer casualties. There were tens of thousands of civilian casualties of the conventional wars in Iraq and Afghanistan.

There has been no case that we know of of someone being killed by a drone because the CIA or the Defense Department thought he was a terrorist and he wasn't. No charge of an innocent terrorist. Most of our targets bragged about their plans to kill Americans. There has been no case of: "We got the wrong bunker and hit a bunch of innocents and the bad guys got away."

So, on the record, our government seems to have used drones fairly judiciously. Again, have the recent wars been more productive, rational, or humane? Have they been less bloody than drones?

On the contrary.

Drones Spare American Soldiers

Every time a drone takes out a terrorist leader, and maybe a few of his henchmen, that is a firefight saved. That is precious young American life saved. And that's a very good thing.

We will always need conventional soldiers. But the last two wars have shown us that conventional warfare has limited potential for success in today's world.

Drones are a tool in a new kind of warfare.

No form of war is decent or moral.

But the aim, in warfare, is to kill as many bad guys as possible and save as many of our guys as possible. Drones further that aim.

A world without war would be a better world. But in war drones are preferable to the massive bombing of Baghdad during the "shock-and-awe" phase of the 10-year war on Iraq; the bombing of hospitals in North Vietnam during that war; the firebombing of Dresden during World War II.

Remember the plot to assassinate Hitler? Suppose it had worked.

Imagine getting Hitler or [Iraqi President] Saddam [Hussein] with a drone.

Many, many American lives and many civilian lives would have been spared.

US Drone Strikes: Beneficial to US Security

Aaron Badway and Cloe Bilodeau

Aaron Badway and Cloe Bilodeau wrote this viewpoint as an assignment while graduate students at the Paul H. Nitze School of Advanced International Studies (SAIS), a division of Johns Hopkins University. Because they were assigned a position to argue, it does not necessarily represent their personal views on the subject.

Since the beginning of the war on terror, drone strikes have presented the most effective way to combat terror. US drone strikes against Islamic militants have the tacit support of the Pakistani and Yemeni governments and are vital to the national security of the US and its allies. While the drone strike program is rightly criticized whenever it leads to civilian casualties, the program is the US' best option to ensure security in the region for five key reasons.

First, drone strikes are necessary. The US faces a real threat from terrorist groups like al-Qaida, which actively recruit individuals in remote areas to attack US citizens. These groups currently kill civilians whom they perceive to be threats to their ideology, while promoting the notion that the US is an enemy of Islam. Further, while the US funds development and capacity building programs in both Pakistan and Yemen, drone strikes ensure these programs can be implemented. They are therefore necessary to US security and complementary to development initiatives aiming to stem terrorism.

Second, drone strikes are effective. Drone attacks in Afghanistan, Pakistan, Yemen and Somalia have killed approximately 3500 militants, including top leaders, and reduced these groups' communication networks and recruitment mechanism. Bin Laden himself stated that al-Qaida would not be able to fight repeated drone strikes against their leadership. In Pakistan, strikes have disrupted threats to the US and reduced the violence of the Pakistani Taliban and al-Qaida. There is no evidence that drone strikes create more terrorism against the US, but a lot of data suggests that drone strikes dismantle militant networks.

The drone program is young, and there is certainly room for reform. Still, drone strikes remain the best option.

Additionally, drone strikes are cost-efficient. The US can now sustain a longer-term presence in remote areas than was not possible using conventional warfare tactics. This poses a blow to terrorists' long-term strategy. The drone program costs around one percent of the US military budget, compared to ground troops or manned aerial vehicles which can cost between six to 42 times more.

Drone strikes also reduce civilian deaths. Drones kill fewer foreign civilians as a percentage of total fatalities than any other military weapon. The New America Foundation estimates civilian casualties caused by drones are around six to 17 percent. This low number has decreased as drones become more precise. Further, drones have reduced terrorist groups' ability to kill civilians in their home countries. Drone strikes are also more humane than relying on the Pakistani or Yemeni militaries, which have a history of unprofessionalism and of human rights violations. Civilians do not flee from drones en masse, but whenever the Yemeni military launches an offensive against terrorist strongholds, civilians leave by the thousands.

For all the strategic and moral benefits of drones, there needs to be greater transparency in their use. The greatest threat is criticism of impunity for the use of drones, and classifying information regarding the program prevents true accountability. The drone program is young, and there is certainly room for reform. Still, drone strikes remain the best option.

Military Drones Reduce Civilian Casualties

Michael W. Lewis

Michael W. Lewis is a law professor at Ohio Northern University.

Mark Bowden's cover story in this month's *The Atlantic* magazine is one of the best things I've seen written on drones in the past several years. The *Black Hawk Down* author's descriptions and takeaways on most aspects of the drone program are consistent with my own experience in military aviation and the information I have gathered from human rights organizations, drone operators, military lawyers, senior military, and CIA personnel who have run the drone programs, as well as from senior military policy advisors who were involved in changing the way drones are used.

Perhaps most importantly, his description of the drone operator's reaction—one of shock and uncertainty—to performing a specific mission clearly undermines the widely circulated but exceptionally irresponsible criticism that drones have created a "Playstation mentality" among their operators. An additional fact that the article did not include, but that has been understood (although not widely reported) for several years now, is that drone operators suffer from PTSD [post-traumatic stress disorder]-like symptoms at rates similar to—and sometimes greater than—those experienced by combat forces on the ground. It turns out that even from 8,000 miles away, taking human life and graphically observing your handiwork is nothing like playing a video game.

Michael W. Lewis, "Guest Post: Do Drones Cause Fewer Civilian Casualties Than Traditional Combat?," *Opinio Juris*, August 23, 2013. OpinioJuris.org. Copyright © 2013 Opinio Juris. All rights reserved. Reproduced with permission.

Focus on Civilian Casualties

Another highlight is his treatment of the question of civilian casualties. All armed conflicts cause civilian casualties, and most modern conflicts have done so in large numbers, in part due to the fact that insurgents often hide among the civilian population. The 2006 Israeli conflict with Hezbollah and its 2009 and 2012 battles with Hamas in Gaza, the 1999 Russian war with Chechen rebels, and the final stages of the struggle between Sri Lanka and the LTTE (Tamil Tigers) all killed more civilians than combatants, in some cases substantially more. Although the U.S. has not caused civilian casualties at rates that high, there have been memorable examples of civilian casualties in each of the recent conflicts in which we have been involved, and those casualties were caused by all kinds of weapons systems. The 1991 Gulf War had the Al-Firdos bunker airstrike that killed up to 400 civilians. The Kosovo campaign included airstrikes that hit the Chinese Embassy in Belgrade and struck a civilian train in the Grdelica gorge. The 2003 Iraq War included civilian casualties caused by Marine ground troops in Haditha and military contractors in Nisoor Square, while a cruise missile strike in 2009 killed approximately 35 civilians at al-Majalah in Yemen.

[The] potential of drones to vastly reduce civilian casualties was not fully realized at first, but it has been dramatically attained in the past few years.

Better Intelligence, Better Results

Like any other weapon, drones have caused civilian casualties. But they also have the potential to dramatically reduce civilian casualties in armed conflicts, and particularly in counterinsurgencies. Their ability to follow targets for days or weeks accomplishes two things that contribute to saving the lives of innocents: First, it confirms that the target is engaged in the behavior that put them on the target list, reducing the likelihood of striking someone based on faulty intelligence. Second, by establishing a "pattern of life" for the intended target, it allows operators to predict when the target will be sufficiently isolated to allow a strike that is unlikely to harm civilians.

Another feature that reduces civilian casualties is that drones are controlled remotely, so the decision to employ a weapon can be reviewed in real time by lawyers, intelligence analysts, and senior commanders without any concern (in most cases) that a hesitation to act may cost lives. Even more importantly, the operators themselves are not concerned for their own safety, eliminating the possibility that the combination of tension, an unexpected occurrence, and a concern for personal safety leads to weapons being fired when they shouldn't be.

This potential of drones to vastly reduce civilian casualties was not fully realized at first, but it has been dramatically attained in the past few years.

In 2007, the U.S. Army and Marine Corps began disseminating the COIN Manual that emphasized the need for soldiers to be involved in nation-building and bolstering local civil-society institutions, in addition to defeating insurgents militarily. Part of implementing this strategy involved minimizing civilian casualties. When Gen. Stanley McChrystal took command of ISAF in Afghanistan in 2009, he emphasized the need to continue reducing civilian casualties in all phases of operations. He assigned teams of civilians and military officers to conduct root-cause analysis of every civilian casualty in theater and tasked them with developing protocols to eliminate such deaths.

Targeting Vehicles, Not Compounds, Reduces Collateral Damage

These teams produced a number of recommendations for drones. One of the most significant was switching the preferred method of targeting from compounds to vehicles. While targeting compounds improved the likelihood that the right individual was being targeted, it also greatly increased the chances that members of the target's family and the families of his bodyguards and close associates would be harmed. Although vehicle strikes ran a greater risk of target misidentification, increasing surveillance and pattern-of-life analysis mitigated that risk. Because it is easier to determine who is in a vehicle than to keep track of everyone who enters and leaves a compound, vehicle strikes reduced the likelihood that family members and friends would be collateral damage. Also, because vehicle strikes can be conducted on isolated roads, the likelihood of other civilian bystanders being harmed was minimized.

There can be no question that drones as they are currently operated are the ideal counterinsurgency weapon.

How do we know that this has succeeded? Bowden mentions studies done by several independent organizations that have assessed civilian casualties caused by drones in Pakistan. The three most well respected and independent sources on this issue are the *Long War Journal,* the New America Foundation and The Bureau of Investigative Journalism (TBIJ). Among these, the U.K.-based TBIJ has consistently produced the highest estimates of civilian casualties for drone strikes. According to TBIJ, between January 2012 and July 2013, there were approximately 65 drone strikes in Pakistan, which they estimate to have killed a minimum of 308 people. Yet of these casualties, even TBIJ estimates that only 4 were civilians (that number has been revised down from 7 in the past month or so). This would amount to a civilian casualty rate of less than 1.5 percent, meaning that only 1 in 65 casualties caused by drones over that 19-month period was a civilian. This speaks to drone-effective discrimination between civilian and military targets that no other weapons system can possibly match.

Critics Have Faulty Arguments

In spite of this success, there are many critics that continue to claim that drones are illegal, immoral and/or ineffective, largely because they cause too many civilian casualties and thereby create more enemies than they eliminate. Most such claims are backed by references to the total aggregate TBIJ numbers to demonstrate how many total civilians have been killed by drones since 2007, but the drones' performance over the last year and a half is always ignored. Others are backed by anecdotal evidence like the Senate testimony of a Yemeni activist, Farea al-Muslimi who claimed that his personal research indicates that the vast majority of those killed by drones in Yemen were civilians. However his methodology, asking friends and family members of the victims if the dead were AQAP [al Qaeda in the Arabian Peninsula], leaves much to be desired in terms of rigor.

There may be questions about whether the armed conflict approach is the right one to take against insurgent groups like core al Qaeda, AQAP or AQIM [al Qaeda in the Islamic Maghreb] (and given their success when not opposed by substantial military force, those questions should answer themselves), but there can be no question that drones as they are currently operated are the ideal counterinsurgency weapon. Any argument that drones cause too many civilian casualties to be effective in counterinsurgency operations, essentially concludes that counterinsurgency operations cannot succeed.

Military Drones Can Help Protect Human Rights

Kristin Bergtora Sandvik and Kjersti Lohne

Kristin Bergtora Sandvik is a senior researcher at the Peace Research Institute Oslo and director of the Norwegian Centre for Humanitarian Studies. Her research focuses on the relationships between international law, humanitarianism, technology, and violence. Kjersti Lohne is an academic visitor at Oxford and a PhD research fellow at the University of Oslo.

This article explores and attempts to define the emerging concept of the humanitarian drone by critically examining actual and anticipated transfers of unmanned aerial vehicles (UAVs), or drones, from the global battlespace to the humanitarian emergency zone. . . .

In recent years, the humanitarian cost of the drone wars has become the focus of international attention. Much less visibly, terms such as *humanitarian drones, drone humanitarianism, drones for human rights* and *humanitarian missiles* have been migrating from the far corners of the blogosphere into mainstream discussions of humanitarian action and humanitarian policy. As the 'humanitarian drone' gains currency as a political concept, it is important to disentangle the ideas from which that concept has emerged, and to think about the implications for humanitarian action. In this article, we do so by considering a range of actual and projected transfers of unmanned aerial vehicles (UAVs, hereinafter also *drones*) from the global battlefield to the humanitarian emergency zone.

Kristin Bergtora Sandvik and Kjersti Lohne, "Drones for Global Justice: Implications for the Humanitarian Enterprise," in "The Rise of the Humanitarian Drone: Giving Content to an Emerging Concept," *Millennium Journal of International Studies*, June 27, 2014. Copyright © 2014 Sage Publications Ltd. All rights reserved. Reproduced with permission.

Under a well-established definition, the term *humanitarian assistance* refers to aid and action designed to save lives, alleviate suffering, and maintain and protect human dignity during and in the aftermath of emergencies. As an analytical starting point, the concept of the humanitarian drone can be understood as a set of contested representations of technology, and technological functions, intended to meet some of these assistance needs.

Just as drones have rapidly become intrinsic to modern warfare, it appears that they will increasingly find their place as part of the humanitarian governance apparatus.

Over the past decade, the close relationship between military action and humanitarian aid during international engagements in Afghanistan, Iraq, Haiti and Libya has led to debates about the nature and ends of the humanitarian enterprise. Although the geographies of war and humanitarian aid have always overlapped—at least since the battle of Solferino in 1859, which ultimately led to the founding of the International Red Cross—what has changed are the ways in which armed conflict, humanitarian interventions and humanitarian aid operations intersect as fields of global governance, spanning both war and disaster zones.

The Global Battlefield

The concept of the 'global battlefield' or the 'global battlespace', which originated in US military doctrine and refers to the multidimensional nature of modern warfare, is gaining increasing currency. As a conceptual and material project, war is now 'everywhere', woven into the matrix of contemporary social life. Within the global battlespace, Predators (General Atomics, United States), Herons (IAI, Israel) and Watchkeepers (Thales, France) provide intelligence for armed attacks or occupation, while MQ-9 Reapers (also General Atomics) and

Hermes 450s (Elbit Systems, Israel) are deployed to eliminate individuals identified as insurgents or terrorists. The cargo drone Kaman K-Max (Lockheed Martin and Kaman Aerospace, US) supplies troops to remote outposts in Afghanistan. Interconnecting with the global battlespace is a humanitarian emergency zone, where a global system of international organisations, donor and troop-contributing nations, and nongovernmental organisations (NGOs) operate in parallel with and across domestic state structures to respond to and administer a permanent condition of crisis.

Just as drones have rapidly become intrinsic to modern warfare, it appears that they will increasingly find their place as part of the humanitarian governance apparatus. What opportunities do drones offer for humanitarian governance? How will drones change humanitarian practices and, by extension, the humanitarian profession? We consider the notion of the humanitarian drone as it has recently surfaced in two different types of discourse: (1) as a way of labelling technical and logistical humanitarian functions a drone might potentially fulfill, such as providing better data on unfolding crises or ongoing human rights violations, delivering aid to victims in hard-to-get locations, or supporting a responsibility-to-protect (R2P) mandate; and (2) as a way of describing ethically desirable uses to which drones might be put, such as enhancing the understanding of assistance needs, making aid more effective, and ending human rights violations.

We expect that the use of drones will permeate the humanitarian field, and that the drones will be operated not only by states or intergovernmental actors, but also by [nongovernmental organizations].

Our goal is to analyse these two types of discourse and their broader implications for humanitarian action. Although we recognise the potent force of humanitarianism as a discourse in global governance, and as a popular 'transnational concern to help persons in exceptional distress', humanitarian action is here conceived broadly as material, political and military responses—by the humanitarian arms of the United Nations (UN), international NGOs, and states—to particular invocations of humanitarian suffering. Significantly, as used here, this form of 'humanitarian reason' is claimed as the prerogative of liberal democracies. We situate our discussion of the rise of the humanitarian drone in the context of two observations regarding current thinking on technology and crisis, both of which we address critically in the course of the article: (1) optimism about the possibility of using technology to improve humanitarian action (including mitigating the increasing insecurity of humanitarian workers), and (2) the idea that more precise weapons technology is 'humanising' warfare.

The Military-to-Civilian Transfer

Many of the technological innovations in question are the outcomes of military-civilian transfer—thus, they are so-called dual-use technologies, which can be used for both peaceful and military aims. While there is a dearth of scholarly focus on the 'turn to technology' in humanitarian action, the rich literature on technological transformations and politics can help bridge the gap. Our argument is based on two assumptions about drones as a purported form of humanitarian technology: first, technology is not neutral, that is, instead of society passively adopting technology, technology and society engage in a mutually constitutive relationship. Thus, the construction of technology is subject to political contestation and to the realities of professionalism, finance and politics; nevertheless, in keeping with Daniel R. McCarthy's reflections on technological determinism, the diffusion of non-human objects 'generates new political settlements', which, in themselves, constitute a form of institutional power. As evidenced by the ongoing drone wars, UAV technology enables a specific set of political and military rationales and projects that must be examined—not for their oft-cited 'newness' but for the power they represent.

Our second assumption is as follows: although UAV technology may still be relatively primitive, it will evolve and proliferate as a technological paradigm. Consequently, we expect that the use of drones will permeate the humanitarian field, and that the drones will be operated not only by states or intergovernmental actors, but also by NGOs. So far, however, the implications of this proliferation and use for humanitarian action have barely begun to be recognised, and no critical attention has been given to how the humanitarian use of drones is framed and discussed—or by whom. . . .

The humanitarian drone should be understood, at least in part, as a war dividend flowing from military spending on the war on terror.

We argue that this process should be understood not merely as a mechanical transfer of hardware, but also as the transfer of social, cultural and political practices. In our account of the humanitarian drone, the military and the humanitarian fields are enmeshed—politically, materially and socially. Hence, any humanitarian use of drones must be read in the context of their origin as military technologies. . . .

Making Sense of the Humanitarian Drone

This article attempts to make sense of the emergence of the humanitarian drone as a political concept by subjecting UAV technology, and the ideas that have formed around it, to some much-needed scrutiny. We are particularly concerned about the potential consequences for humanitarian discourse and the humanitarian enterprise. In our view, a focus on weaponised drones fails to capture the transformative potential of humanitarian drones and their possible impact on humanitarian action, and the associated pitfalls.

The starting point for our investigation is the emerging assumption that drones will change the humanitarian enterprise for the better. To explain the rise of the concept of the humanitarian drone, we note that the humanitarian enterprise embraces the idea of improving humanitarian action through technology. We further suggest that the humanitarian drone should be understood, at least in part, as a war dividend flowing from military spending on the war on terror. Importantly, just as the humanitarian enterprise has been identified as a significant market for UAVs, the humanitarian ethos has become an important commodity for drone manufacturers. Hence, it is important to attend to the strong commercial logic underpinning the promotion of the humanitarian drone. It is equally important to be aware of the ways in which drone use may shift humanitarian agendas and the political and financial priorities of governments (who tend to be protective of domestic defence contractors), international organisations and NGOs. Also of note is the industry's attempt to forge a moral economy based on a shared humanitarian logic that is, in part, embraced by a humanitarian enterprise that holds firm to the belief that adding technology automatically generates progress.

In addition to predicting that military rationales and practices will travel with drones used for humanitarian purposes, we propose that existing tensions between the military and the humanitarian fields will shape how the humanitarian drone is used to mediate and respond to human suffering. . . .

Many Questions Left to Ask

We would like to conclude by indicating where we think more research is needed. First, we encourage international relations scholars to follow the money: what is the political economy of humanitarian drones? How do the development and marketing of new prototypes correspond to regulatory efforts, and with the ways in which UAV procurements are processed, labelled and legitimated by governments and international organisations? Second, given the increasing use of drone technology in civilian airspace, it is essential to examine the political meanings surrounding representations of all categories and uses of drones—from human rights drones, to eco drones, anti-poaching drones, agro drones, and so forth. How do other types of drones, and the work they do, compare with the idea of the humanitarian drone? Third, returning to our argument that practices travel with hardware, sound empirical research is needed to explore not only how humanitarian drone practices are enacted, and by whom, but also how this novel form of humanitarian praxis is experienced and interpreted by those at the receiving end.

Military Drone Use Makes War More Likely

Lauren McCauley

Lauren McCauley is a staff writer for Common Dreams, a news and opinion website for the progressive community.

The embrace of killer drones by the United States government is likely to increase anti-U.S. sentiment, erode national sovereignty and trigger a "slippery slope" into endless war, a prominent military and intelligence panel warned in a new report published Thursday [June 26, 2014].

Recommendations and Report of the Task Force on United States Drone Policy is the result of a year-long study by a high-level task force of military, intelligence and foreign policy experts assembled by the nonpartisan Stimson Center.

In the report, the panel warns that the proliferation of killer drones as a "pillar of U.S. counterterrorism strategy" has enabled policies that "likely would not have been adopted in the absence of UAVs [Unmanned Aerial Vehicles]," particularly the "extraordinarily broad" interpretation of the Authorization for Use of Military Force, or AUMF.

Echoing the concerns of many anti-war groups, the panel notes that the increasing use of lethal drones "may create a slippery slope leading to continual or wider wars."

The report continues:

> The seemingly low-risk and low-cost missions enabled by UAV technologies may encourage the United States to fly such missions more often, pursuing targets with UAVs that would be deemed not worth pursuing if manned aircraft or special operation forces had to be put at risk.

UAVs also create an escalation risk insofar as they may lower the bar to enter a conflict, without increasing the likelihood of a satisfactory outcome.

The panel says that the United States' unilateral targeting of individuals in foreign sovereign states "may encourage other states to follow suit with their own military platforms or commercial entities."

The report argues that the use of drones in an "unprecedented and expanding way" raises significant strategic, legal and ethical questions.

Risks Are Many, Benefits Few

Among the strategic risks, the group argues that "blowback" from civilian casualties may "increase anti-U.S. sentiment and become a potent recruiting tool for terrorist organizations."

Further, the panel says that the United States' unilateral targeting of individuals in foreign sovereign states "may encourage other states to follow suit with their own military platforms or commercial entities."

Citing the failure on the part of the American government to carry out a thorough analysis weighing the costs and benefits of continuing their drone war, the report concedes: "There is no indication that a U.S. strategy to destroy Al Qaeda has curbed the rise of Sunni Islamic extremism, deterred the establishment of Shia Islamic extremist groups or advanced long-term U.S. security interests."

Despite this, and the panel's criticisms regarding the U.S. government's lack of transparency and the risks inherent in the use of drones, the report concludes on the assumption that killer drones will continue to be a fundamental tool in military operations.

Thus, the panel issued the below list of recommendations, quoted from the report, to shape and guide U.S. drone policy:

1. Conduct a strategic review of the role of lethal UAVs in targeted counterterrorism strikes;

2. Improve transparency in targeted UAV strikes;

3. Transfer general responsibility for carrying out lethal UAV strikes from the CIA to the military;

4. Develop more robust oversight and accountability mechanisms for targeted strikes outside of hot battle-fields;

5. Foster the development of appropriate international norms for the use of lethal force outside traditional battlefields;

6. Assess UAV-related technological developments and likely future trends, and create an interagency research and development strategy geared toward advancing US national security interests in a manner consistent with US values;

7. Review and reform UAV-related export control rules and FAA rules, with a view to minimizing unnecessary regulatory burdens on the development of the US UAV industry, while still safeguarding US national security interests and ensuring responsible UAV development and use; and

8. Accelerate the FAA's efforts to meet the requirements of the 2012 FAA Reauthorization Bill.

Responding to the report's release, Steve Vladeck, co-editor in chief of the *Just Security* blog, who was part of one of the "working groups" that gave informal advice to the task force, wrote: "Folks won't necessarily agree with all of its recommendations (or believe that they go far enough), but given the Task Force's bipartisan, high-level composition, its recommendations will be ignored at its readers' peril."

Military Drone Strikes Violate Human Rights

Deborah Dupre

Deborah Dupre has been a human rights, environmental, and peace activist for more than thirty years.

As other nations are having popular revolutions to strengthen human rights, former US president Jimmy Carter says the United States government counterterrorism policies are clearly violating at least 10 of the 30 articles of the Universal Declaration of Human Rights and that drone strikes and targeted assassinations see the nation violating rights in a way that "abets our enemies and alienates our friends."

"Revelations that top officials are targeting people to be assassinated abroad, including American citizens, are only the most recent, disturbing proof of how far our nation's violation of human rights has extended," writes the 39th president in the *New York Times* on Monday, June 25, 2012. Carter's critical Op Ed, *A Cruel and Unusual Record*, states that "with all the revolution sweeping around the world, America should 'make the world safer.' Instead, however, 'America's violaton of international human rights abets our enemies and alienates our friends.'"

In 1948, with US leadership, the Universal Declaration of Human Rights was adopted as "the foundation of freedom, justice and peace in the world." It was a clear commitment that power would no longer serve as a cover to oppress or injure people. The core principle behind each of the 30 articles of the declaration is equal rights. The articles detail the

Declaration's equal rights of all people to life, liberty, security, protection of law and freedom from torture, arbitrary detention and forced exile.

"US's government counterterrrorism policies are now clearly violating at least 10 of the 30 articles written in the Universal Declaration of Human Rights," Carter wrote. "As a result, our country can no longer speak with moral authority on these critical issues."

Investigations indicate that a large part of the drone casualties were civilian and that numbers have increased dramatically since Barack Obama assumed the presidency.

War Crimes "un-American"

Carter's Op Ed regarding the US abandoning its role as the global champion of human rights appeared less than a week after the UN released a report on US drone strikes to "combat terrorism." On June, 21, 2012, UN rapporteur on extrajudicial killings, summary or arabitrary executions, Christof Heyns asserted that the US needs to be held legally accountable for using armed drones, possibly involving war crimes. If it is true, he said, that "there have been secondary drone strikes on rescuers who are helping (the injured) after an initial drone attack, those further attacks are a war crime."

A second UN rapporteur, Ben Emmerson QC, who monitors counter-terrorism, stated that protection of the ultimate human right, the right to life, required countries to establish independent inquiries into each US drone killing. While the US is not a signatory to the International Criminal Court (ICC) nor many other international legal forums where legal action could begin, it is part of the International Court of Justice (ICJ) where one nation state can initiate a case against another.

While a definitive number of drone victims remains publicly unknown, the American Civil Liberties Union (ACLU) estimated that approximately 4,000 people fell victim to US drone raids between 2002 and 2011 in Yemen, Pakistan and Somalia alone. (Drone strikes threaten 50 years of international law, says UN, Owen Bowcott, *The Guardian*, 21 June 2012.) Most drone casualties were civilian and those murders increased dramatically after Barack Obama became president, according to independent investigations. Threatening 50 years of international law, Obama has stated drones are his "weapon of choice," according to a now deleted *Washington Post* article quoted by this author. (CIA drones intolerable says Pakistan, despite Obama's 'weapon of choice', Examiner.com, 10 Oct. 2011.) The *Washington Post* later referred to drones being Obama's "go-to weapon" in Eugene Robinson's OpEd, President Obama's immoral drone war (2 Dec. 2012). US drone attacks "are killing innocent civilians in a way that is obscene and immoral," Robinson opined. Concurring with human rights defenders globally, he stated, "I'm afraid that ignoring this ugly fact makes Americans complicit in murder."

Human rights group Reprieve brought to light that the official Pentagon term for a drone victim is "Bugsplat." (Rare photos of CIA drone "Bugsplat" bodies in secret blackhole battle released, D. Dupré, *Examiner*, 14 Dec. 2011.) North Waziristan resident Noor Behram worked with Reprieve charity organization's founding director Stafford Smith. Behram spent years photographing drone strike aftermaths, often at personal risk.

"I want to show taxpayers in the Western world what their tax money is doing to people in another part of the world: killing civilians, innocent victims, children," Behram said. (Rare photos of CIA drone "Bugsplat" bodies in secret blackhole battle released.)

In 2014, using Bureau of Investigative Journalism reports, Reprieve examined cases in which specific people were targeted by drones multiple times. Those data raised questions about accuracy of US intelligence "guiding strikes" that American officials describe with words such as "clinical" and "precise." Reporting on Reprieve's findings, *The Guardian* stated that "even when operators target specific individuals—the most focused effort of what Barack Obama calls 'targeted killing'—they kill vastly more people than their targets, often needing to strike multiple times." Attempts to assassinate 41 men resulted in killing an estimated 1,147 people. (*The Guardian*, 24 Nov. 2014.) While it is unknown precisely how many hundreds of innocent civilians US drone attacks have killed, each strike and death was approved by Washington's highest authorities, unthinkable before the Obama regime.

Three days before Carter's harsh criticism of Obama's drone human rights abuses, in a Huffington Post Blog, former US Senator Fritz Hollings of South Carolina declared killing by drone "un-American":

"I've been an American for 90 years and drone killing is un-American. It's an excellent weapon to use in a war, but not to declare war. Article I, Section 8 of the Constitution reserves the declaration of war for the Congress—not the President, not the CIA, not the Defense Department. Already we have a dispute in Pakistan where the Ambassador has the authority of the US but the authority is now being used by the CIA. I know about the authority of Congress a week after 9/11 to hunt down and capture or eliminate terrorists. I voted for it. But having worked on the Defense Budget for 38 years, I didn't contemplate drone killing. We had never heard of drones. We were looking for Osama bin Laden and the crew that devastated the World Trade Towers. The majority of this crew was from Saudi Arabia. We have never used drones in Saudi Arabia, but are now drone killing in Yemen and Somalia that are no threat to the US. In America we are able to face our accuser and defend ourselves." (Sen. Fritz Hollings, Former US senator [D-SC], *Un-American*, 22 June 2012)

"Targeted Individuals" Claim Surveillance and Attacks

Media and rights advocates' attention to drone abuse is welcomed by thousands of innocent individuals in the US struggling to survive government-sponsored covert assaults that escalated under the Obama administration with the president's "Targeted Killings," his political lingo for assassinations. In the US, a cohort of thousands of innocent victims known as Targeted Individuals (TIs), including many reputable professionals and other credible victims, consistently allege being kept under constant surveillance and covertly attacked, some by unmanned aerial technologies and most by cyber-terrorism—Internet hacking. Many of these TIs provide evidence that law enforcement refuses to protect them from these attacks. [The American Civil Liberties Union] ACLU investigations later found that police involved in spying on and targeting Americans are called rakers. (*Are You a Targeted Individual? Foolproof Research Criteria Secrets*, D. Dupré, Before It's News, 28 July 2015.)

This law violates the right to freedom of expression and to be presumed innocent until proved guilty, two other rights enshrined in the declaration.

Recent laws allow "unprecedented violations of our rights to privacy through warrantless wiretapping and government mining of our electronic communications," Carter stated. He called for Washington to "reverse course and regain moral leadership."

"While the country has made mistakes in the past, the widespread abuse of human rights over the last decade has been a dramatic change from the past."

The Universal Declaration of Human Rights "has been invoked by human rights activists and the international community to replace most of the world's dictatorships with democracies and to promote the rule of law in domestic and global affairs," Carter stated. "It is disturbing that, instead of strengthening these principles, our government's counterterrorism policies are now clearly violating at least 10 of the declaration's 30 articles, including the prohibition against 'cruel, inhuman or degrading treatment or punishment.'"

Expanded Presidential Powers

Beginning with the George W. Bush regime's USA PATRIOT ACT, during the Barack Obama regime, legislation legalized the president's right to detain a person indefinitely on suspicion of affiliation with terrorist organizations or "associated forces," Carter reminded the public, referring to the National Defense Authorization Act (NDAA 2012). "This law violates the right to freedom of expression and to be presumed innocent until proved guilty, two other rights enshrined in the declaration," Carter wrote.

Terrorism and Counterterrorism Program senior counsel for Human Rights Watch, Andrea Prasow had previously asserted that "mandatory military detention is what martial-law states do, not democracies," as the *New York Times* reported just before Obama signed the NDAA into law, codifying martial law. Prasow called the mandatory detention provision an "outrageous" undermining of prosecutorial discretion. (Martial law provision secretly passed in Congress Committee, Deborah Dupré, Examiner.com, June 25, 2011.)

There are "unprecedented violations of our rights to privacy through warrantless wiretapping and government mining of our electronic communications," Carter continued. "Popular state laws permit detaining individuals because of their appearance, where they worship or with whom they associate."

Instead of making the world safer, "America's violation of international human rights abets our enemies and alienates our friends," Carter said. . . .

Human Rights Remain a Concern

Instead of fostering human rights, the US is rapidly changing from "One nation under God," as stated in the US Pledge of Allegiance, to One nation under drones. Congress passed legislation for what the Federal Aviation Authority (FAA) predicted approximately 30,000 drones in operation in US skies by 2020 and the targeting of human rights defenders is predicted to increase. Spy drones, commercially available for less than $1,000, are barely different from those police departments use to spy on the public. In August 2015, North Dakota has become the first state to authorize weaponized drones in the US.

In Africa, then Secretary of State and at the time of this writing [September 2015], presidential hopeful Hillary Clinton spoke openly about the US's need to improve drone capabilities. Clinton was in Uganda speaking to president Yoweri Museveni and surveying US drones used by the Ugandan military in Somalia to reportedly fight al-Qaeda-linked militants.

"Now we have to figure out how we can see through thick vegetation to find [Ugandan guerilla leader] Joseph Kony," she said, referring to the controversial "Kony 2012" documentary propaganda film that had over 92 million views about capturing fabled enemy Joseph Kony. Analysts say that the film was created to spur widespread outrage and manipulate support for the US to invade Africa. It depicted Kony as a ruthless African warlord who would kidnap children, butcher victims, and take women as sex slaves. . . .

In her memoir, *Hard Choices*, Clinton defends the Obama regime's drone targeted assassinations. In chapter 9, Clinton says drone strikes quickly became "one of the most effective and controversial elements of the Obama Administration's strategy against al Qaeda and like-minded terrorists." She defends the careful planning of drone strikes. Hundreds of dead babies and children drone victims alone have proven Clinton's statements to be unfounded or untrue. Drone propaganda and censorship, however, continue. . . .

While not legally binding, the June 2012 UN report on drones "escalates the volume of international concerns" over "the Obama administration's weapon of choice against Al Qaeda and its allies," the *New York Times* reported. Jim Galloway, political insider of the *Atlanta Journal Constitution* summarized Carter's stinging *New York Times* Op Ed piece: "Jimmy Carter isn't too thrilled with the idea of President Barack Obama . . . picking individual winners and losers in the war on terror."

A 2014 report, "Testing Theories of American Politics: Elites, Interest Groups, and Average Citizens," showed findings of a peer-reviewed study at Princeton and Northwestern Universities that the US is not a democracy based on human rights. It is, according to the major report, an "oligarchy" in which the US government meets demands of the wealthy, whereas desires and rights of everyone else are ignored. Drones are indeed an "effective tool" for this end.

America's Foreign Drone Strike Program Lacks Transparency

Matthew Spurlock

Matthew Spurlock is a legal fellow at the American Civil Liberties Union's National Security Project.

Targeted killings have been a central part of U.S. national security strategy for more than a decade, but the American public still knows scandalously little about who the government kills, and why. Today we're filing a new lawsuit in our continuing fight to fix that.

The CIA and the military use drones to target suspected "militants," "insurgents," and "terrorists" in at least half a dozen countries. American drone strikes have killed thousands of people abroad, many of them children. The program has engendered pervasive fear and anger against the United States in countries where the attacks frequently occur.

Our government's deliberative and premeditated killings—and the many more civilian deaths from the strikes—raise profound legal and ethical questions that ought to be the subject of public debate. The Obama administration has made numerous promises of greater transparency and oversight on drones. In his 2013 State of the Union address, President Obama pledged to make lethal targeting "more transparent to the American people and the world" because "in our democracy, no one should just take my word for it that we're doing things the right way."

But the administration has failed to follow through on these commitments to openness, and it is continuing to withhold basic information. When it has released anything—or been compelled to by lawsuits—discussion of crucial aspects of the program have been omitted or redacted. This lack of transparency makes the public reliant on the government's self-serving and sometimes false representations about the targeted-killing program.

That's why today the ACLU filed a new lawsuit to enforce a Freedom of Information Act request asking for basic information on the program, including records on how the government picks targets, before-the-fact assessments of potential civilian casualties, and "after-action" investigations into who was actually killed.

[The US government] chooses to keep nearly all the details about how the [drone] program works hidden from view.

The ACLU has made some headway for transparency. We are litigating two other FOIA lawsuits seeking information about targeted killings. One of them is about the strikes that killed three Americans in Yemen: Anwar al-Aulaqi, his 16-year old son Abdulrahman, and Samir Khan. Despite the public promises of openness, the government has continued to fight tooth-and-nail against releasing documents in those cases—or in some instances, even admitting that it has any documents at all.

In both cases we have won important rulings in federal appeals courts, forcing the government to release some documents, including a 41-page Justice Department Office of Legal Counsel memo addressing the legal theories that were the basis for the extrajudicial killing of Anwar al-Aualqi. The belated publication of the memo was an important victory for transparency, which led to a broad and long-overdue debate about the lawfulness of the government's targeted-killing program and, in particular, of the lawfulness of the government's deliberate and pre-meditated killing of a U.S. citizen. But the memo—almost a third of which was redacted—leaves many questions unanswered.

For example, the memo doesn't explain the government's definition of imminence, the circumstances that would make "capture infeasible" (and therefore, according to the government, lethal targeting permissible), or the reasons for the government's targeting decisions. Worse, it point(s) to a whole body of secret law that the administration continues to shield from the American public.

The administration's subsequent gestures towards transparency are just as scant. The public summary of the secret *Presidential Policy Guidance*—which sets new standards for lethal targeting—relies on the same conclusory definitions as the Office of Legal Counsel memo. In a major speech at the National Defense University in 2013, the president asserted that "before any strike is taken, there must be near-certainty that no civilians will be killed or injured—the highest standard we can set." But multiple investigative reports contradict this assurance. The government could dispute these findings, but instead it chooses to keep nearly all the details about how the program works hidden from view.

We aren't giving up. One of the most important aspects of our new lawsuit is that it covers more recent documents, including the Presidential Policy Guidance under which the targeted killing program likely now operates.

The government's drone program lives far too deep in the shadows. As long as the government continues its campaign of secret, unacknowledged lethal strikes across the globe, we will fight to subject this policy to the scrutiny and debate it deserves.

The Dangerous Seduction of Drones

Medea Benjamin

Medea Benjamin is the founder of the international human rights organization Global Exchange and the antiwar group Code Pink. She is the author of the recent book Drone Warfare: Killing by Remote Control.

Senior [President Barack] Obama administration officials say our government is sharply scaling back its drone strikes in Pakistan. That's a step in the right direction. It would be even better if the entire U.S. program of targeted killings in Pakistan, Yemen, and Somalia were scrapped.

By embracing drones as a primary foreign policy tool, President Barack Obama has taken on the role of prosecutor, judge, jury, and executioner.

Without declaring a war there, U.S. forces have hit Pakistan with more than 350 drones strikes since 2004. These U.S.-engineered operations have left a death toll of somewhere between 2,500 and 3,500 people, including almost 200 children.

Despite being billed as a weapon of precision, only 2 percent of those killed in these drone strikes have been high-level Taliban or al-Qaeda operatives. Most have been either innocent people or low-level militants.

Simply put, our drones have killed young men with scant ability—or intent—to attack Americans. And drones don't just kill people, they terrorize entire communities with their constant buzzing and hovering overhead.

A Stanford/NYU Law School study called *Living Under Drones* shows how the mere presence of drones disrupts community life. Parents grow too afraid to send their children to school or remain in their own homes. They're afraid—with good reason—to attend community gatherings, or go to weddings or funerals.

With every drone strike, more and more join the ranks of al-Qaeda to seek revenge.

"Your government is terrifying 250,000 people in my province to get one or two individuals, who could easily be captured," a young woman leader named Entisar Ali told me in Yemen during my trip there last year. "In your fight against terrorism, you are terrorizing us."

A Powerful Recruiting Tool

By fueling anti-U.S. sentiment, drones also act as a recruiting tool for extremists. In Yemen, when the Obama administration started drone attacks in 2009, there were perhaps 200 people who identified as members of extremist groups. Today, there are over 1,000.

With every drone strike, more and more join the ranks of al-Qaeda to seek revenge. Worldwide, a decade of drone strikes hasn't wiped out al-Qaeda. In fact, al-Qaeda has grown. It now has a larger presence in Syria and Iraq, as well as in several countries in North and West Africa.

If other states were to claim this broad-based authority to kill people anywhere, anytime, using drones "the result would be chaos," explained Philip Alston, a former UN Special Rapporteur on Extrajudicial Executions.

Former Director of National Intelligence Dennis Blair has called drones "dangerously seductive" because they make the government feel it has a strategy for combating terrorism yet really only move the focal point from one place to another and guarantee a perpetual state of war.

A New Arms Race

Finally, drones are dangerous because they are fueling a new arms race. As of today, only the United States, the UK, and Israel have used weaponized drones, but there is already a multibillion-dollar arms race going on. Israel is the No. 1 drones exporter, followed by the United States and China. Over 80 nations possess some form of drones, mostly for surveillance purposes. Between 10 and 15 nations are working on weaponizing their drones.

Another factor fueling the proliferation of armed drones is a global push to make smaller weapons that can be tailored to fit smaller aircraft. This will make it easier for non-state actors like al-Qaeda to get their hands on these types of weapons.

After 10 years of an unsuccessful policy of remote-control killing, it's time to seek effective solutions that adhere to international law and promote democratic ideals. These include peace talks, alliance-building, treating terrorists as criminals who are arrested and tried, targeted development aid, and empowering women. The drone wars are making us less safe by simply creating new enemies abroad.

CHAPTER 3

Should Domestic Law Enforcement Agencies Be Allowed to Use Drones?

Overview: Drones over America—Public Safety Benefit or "Creepy" Privacy Threat?

Anna Mulrine

Anna Mulrine is a staff writer for the Christian Science Monitor.

Shortly after Alan Frazier became a part-time deputy sheriff in Grand Forks, N.D., the police began looking into the possibility of buying some aircraft to boost their law enforcement capabilities. They wanted some help doing things like finding missing people or carrying out rescues in a region dotted by farmsteads threatened by flooding that wipes out access to roads.

Buying a turbine engine helicopter, however, would cost $25 million, a prohibitive price tag even with 11 law enforcement agencies—eight from North Dakota and three in western Minnesota—willing to share the cost.

So Mr. Frazier, also an assistant professor of aviation at the University of North Dakota (UND), began looking into unmanned aerial vehicles (UAVs) as a possible alternative.

But what appears, on one level, to be a sensible, practical, and affordable solution for local law enforcement—the price tag for a small UAV is about the cost of a tricked-out new police cruiser at $50,000—has run smack into public concerns about yet another high-tech invasion of privacy and the popular image of drones as stealthy weapons used against terrorists.

Nonetheless, the technology's potential benefits in pursuing a raft of public safety measures at relatively low cost have enormous appeal for law enforcement agencies across the country, since President Obama signed a bill last year directing the Federal Aviation Administration (FAA) to further open US airspace to drones for both public and private use.

Even before that, the number of permits, known as certificates of authorization (COAs), that the FAA issued to organizations to fly UAVs more than doubled from 146 in 2009 to 313 in 2011. As of February 2013 there were 327 active COAs.

The growth in drones is big business. Some 50 companies are developing roughly 150 systems . . . ranging from miniature flying mechanical bugs to "Battlestar Galactica"-type hovering unmanned airplanes.

The bulk of these permits go to the US military for training, and the Pentagon expects their numbers to grow considerably in the years to come. According to a March 2011 Pentagon estimate, the Department of Defense will have 197 drones at 105 US bases by 2015.

The US Border Patrol has the country's largest fleet of UAVs for domestic surveillance, including nine Predator drones that patrol regions like the Rio Grande, searching for illegal immigrants and drug smugglers. Unlike the missile-firing Predators used by the Central Intelligence Agency to hunt Al Qaeda operatives and their allies, the domestic version of the aircraft—say, those used by the border patrol—is more typically equipped with night-vision technology and long-range cameras that can read license plates. Groups like the American Civil Liberties Union (ACLU) also complain that these drones have see-through imaging technology similar to those used in airports, as well as facial recognition software tied to federal databases.

The growth in drones is big business. Some 50 companies are developing roughly 150 systems, according to *The Wall Street Journal*, ranging from miniature flying mechanical bugs to "Battlestar Galactica"-type hovering unmanned airplanes. It's an industry expected to reach some $6 billion in US sales by 2016.

Those forecasts notwithstanding, neither the FAA nor the association of UAV operators says it knows how many non-military drones are operating in the United States. The ACLU is seeking that information.

The growth in the development of UAVs by both private companies and the US government has not gone unnoticed, creating a backlash in some communities.

In Seattle last month, community members quashed their city's drone program before it even got started. The program was being considered for search-and-rescue operations and some criminal investigations, but was referred to by protesters as "flying government robots watching their every move."

The president says you can take out American citizens in foreign countries. . . . Well, if you can do that, you can take out somebody here as well.

Mayor Mike McGinn spoke with Police Chief John Diaz, "and we agreed that it was time to end the unmanned aerial vehicle program," the mayor wrote in a statement. The drones were returned to the manufacturer.

Just days earlier, Charlottesville, Va., had become the first city in the country to pass a "no-drone zone" resolution, putting in place a two-year moratorium on the use of drones within Charlottesville limits.

"The big concern for us is that they're going to be everywhere," says John Whitehead, an attorney and president of

The Rutherford Institute, a civil liberties organization in Charlottesville, which launched a preemptive fight against drones before the city council.

The move followed an Obama administration memo justifying the use of drones overseas to kill US citizens suspected of taking part in terrorist activities. "The president says you can take out American citizens in foreign countries," Mr. Whitehead says. "Well, if you can do that, you can take out somebody here as well."

On March 6, Attorney General Eric Holder may have reinforced such fears in testimony before the Senate Judiciary Committee when he refused to rule out the use of armed drones on US soil in an emergency "to protect the homeland."

If it all has an air of hysteria about it—Mr. Holder said there are no plans for the domestic use of armed drones and called the scenario "entirely hypothetical" and unlikely—privacy groups point to California's Alameda County, where officials insisted they wanted drones for search-and-rescue missions. An internal memo that surfaced from the sheriff's department, however, noted the drones could be used for "investigative and tactical surveillance, intelligence gathering, suspicious persons, and large crowd-control disturbances." The county dropped its plans.

The first and only known use of a drone in the arrest of a US citizen occurred in December 2011 in North Dakota, when the Nelson County Sheriff's Department asked to borrow one of the US Customs and Border Protection UAVs. The drone provided a good view of the three sons of the owner of a 3,000-acre farm who were involved in a standoff with law enforcement officers. As a result, police were able to tell that the brothers were unarmed, allowing them to enter the farm and arrest the brothers without the confrontation turning into a shootout.

Whitehead imagines a day when drones equipped with sound cannons, which release painful high-decibel sound waves that cause crowds to disperse, could be dispatched by the government to political protests and used as well to "effectively stifle free speech."

The concern that such technologies can be misused to invade privacy and suppress free speech "is a legitimate fear," says UND's Frazier. "Anytime we increase the technological capabilities of the government there's a justifiable concern there. But I think these fears can be offset by the fact that the drones we're using have very limited capabilities."

FAA regulations stipulate that weaponized drones cannot fly in unrestricted US airspace.

Nevertheless, privacy concerns are what have prompted groups including the nonprofit Electronic Frontier Foundation (EFF) to use the Freedom of Information Act to obtain hundreds of documents from the FAA outlining who has been requesting to use drones in America's skies, and why.

Roughly 40 percent of the drone flight requests submitted to the FAA are from the US military. "They are flying drones pretty regularly—eight hours a day, five days a week—to train pilots so that they will be able to fly drones," says Jessica Lynch, a staff attorney for EFF.

These drones are equipped with infrared scanning capabilities and other surveillance gadgets. "Drones have quite a number of technologies on board, including thermal cameras and the ability to intercept communications," Ms. Lynch says. "If they are training pilots, they are training them in these surveillance tools."

FAA regulations stipulate that weaponized drones cannot fly in unrestricted US airspace. The agency also has specific parameters for law enforcement drones. Law enforcement groups, for example, must maintain visual contact with the drone at all times and must also fly at relatively low altitudes.

These are regulations with which the Grand Forks Sheriff's Department has become familiar in the three years since it began looking into using drones, first establishing an Unmanned Aerial Systems unit as part of the department and then applying for COAs to use the drones. The unit, which went fully operational Feb. 1, has conducted 250 simulated missions, but has yet to use a drone in an operation.

Certification tends to be a lengthy and arduous process, Frazier says, adding that there are also some parameters for usage that are meant to promote safety, but can make it tricky for law enforcement to do its jobs.

One provision, for example, is that the drones can fly only by day. Another early rule was that the police had to give 48 hours' notice if they were going to use the drones.

"It's tough to predict if there is going to be a fire tomorrow, or a bank robbery the day after tomorrow," he says. The department was able to convince the FAA to let it fly the drones on one-hour notice instead.

That said, Frazier understands the public's concerns about the use of drones. For that reason, Grand Forks established a 15-member committee—made up of one-third public safety officials, one-third UND faculty, and one-third community residents—to evaluate the use of drones and to troubleshoot questions and concerns of the public. Every law enforcement action involving the drones is to be reviewed by the committee.

Frazier told committee members that the department did not intend to ask for the ability to use the drones for covert surveillance. "We will not use them to, quote, spy on people," Frazier says. Even if that were the intention, he adds, "These small drones are not particularly robust platforms for covert surveillance. I think the public can't understand that my little UAV can only fly for 15 minutes, can't fly out of my line of sight, and can't fly in greater than 15-knot winds."

Out of concern that average citizens could be filmed by sensors on the aircraft, one of the committee's first acts was to instruct police to post road signs warning the public when UAVs are in use.

As technology becomes cheaper and easier to use, it's tempting to use it all the time.

Yet some of the conversations EFF's Lynch has had with other law enforcement agencies haven't been as reassuring about privacy, she says. "We've talked to police about this, and they've said, 'Well, we're going to fly the drones in public airspace, and if you walk around in public you don't have an expectation of privacy in your movements.'"

"While that might be true for a police officer following you down the street, I don't know if that applies when a drone can fly over and surveil everybody walking down that street for an extended period of time," Lynch says.

"You can make the case that drones are helping law enforcement better do their jobs for less [cost] and we should incorporate it," she adds. "As technology becomes cheaper and easier to use, it's tempting to use it all the time."

That is the fear of Texas state lawmaker Lance Gooden, who in February proposed some of the toughest anti-drone legislation in the country. It would prevent drone operators from collecting images, sounds, and smells—or hovering over any home—without permission.

"Two to four years from now, it'll be impossible to get legislation passed because every law enforcement agency will want drones," says Mr. Gooden. While the drone lobby is growing, it is not as powerful as it will become, he adds.

Currently, his bill has the support of 101 of the 150 members of the state Legislature. But some longtime drone experts say such laws are overkill and could impede growth of technology that is useful and relatively inexpensive.

"The ordinances that have been passed are absolutely absurd," says retired Lt. Gen. David Deptula, the first deputy chief of staff for Intelligence, Reconnaissance, and Surveillance for the US Air Force. "And what's precluded are the very valuable civilian applications in terms of traffic control, firefighting, disaster response, border security, the monitoring of power lines—the list goes on and on."

As for privacy concerns, "I can't think of another way of saying it, but that they are unfounded," Deptula adds. "All you have to do is look up in any major metropolitan city and see the cameras all around. And have they ever heard of satellites? Where do they think Google maps come from?"

Frazier concurs. People with a good zoom lens have better cameras than do his small drones, he adds, pointing out that one of the Grand Forks Sheriff's Department's drones has a simple off-the-shelf Panasonic.

The average GPS-enabled cellphone can now track people and their movements to within a few feet, he notes.

That said, "I understand what people mean when they say it's 'creepy,'" Frazier says. "I value my privacy as much as anyone does—it's very sacred in this country." Even if they could do it legally, law enforcement agencies would be making a big mistake using drones for covert surveillance—for the time being, he adds.

"It would be a fatal mistake at this point. We really need to take a crawl, walk, run approach. To go to covert surveillance brings us to a run," Frazier says of the law enforcement community. "If that means we're not Buck Rogers in the 21st century, we're comfortable with that."

Drones Are Essential Tools for Modern Law Enforcement

Eli Richman

Eli Richman was an editorial intern at Governing *magazine when he wrote this viewpoint.*

When an inmate escaped from jail in Montgomery County, Texas, a few years back, police took to the skies. Montgomery County sits just north of Houston, but the inmate fled into a nearby wooded area, making it harder for law enforcement officers to track him down. Fortunately, the sheriff's department was able to secure a helicopter from the Texas Department of Public Safety. Officers located the inmate using an infrared camera, and they directed deputies to the location.

Today, they'd just use a drone.

Unmanned aerial vehicles, better known as UAVs or drones, are beginning to be embraced by local law enforcement agencies across the United States. Unmanned drones have, of course, made headlines in recent years for their use in foreign military operations. Drone surveillance helped target Osama bin Laden's compound, and a CIA Predator drone fired the missile that killed Anwar al-Awlaki, another high-profile Al Qaeda figure. Now, the vehicles are likely moving into domestic airspace as well. In an effort to push for drone use in police and fire departments, the U.S. Department of Homeland Security (DHS) has reportedly awarded more than $3 million in grants to at least 13 local law enforcement agencies to purchase small drones—including Montgomery County, which last year became one of the first local agencies in the country to acquire its own aerial drone. The county purchased a ShadowHawk MK-II drone last year for about $300,000, using a $220,000 DHS grant.

It's not just police departments that see big potential in unmanned drones. Fire departments and other emergency response teams could use them [as well].

Drones Are a Natural Fit for Police

Drones could revolutionize police work. Helicopters are expensive to fuel and maintain, and flying them takes specialized piloting skills. Because they're in relatively short supply, using a helicopter often requires interdepartmental coordination, as was the case in Montgomery County's manhunt. By comparison, drones are easy. They cost about 100 times less than a helicopter, and operating a drone costs significantly less per hour. They're extremely light: Montgomery's gas-powered ShadowHawk weighs just 49 pounds. At six feet long, it can fit in the back of an SUV, and piloting it requires nothing more than a laptop computer and a remote control. It's a nimble crime-fighting tool that will be an essential asset in the future, says Montgomery Chief Deputy Randy McDaniel. When McDaniel's office acquired the drone last year, he issued a statement saying, "I absolutely believe it will become a critical component on all SWAT callouts and narcotics raids and emergency management operations."

"Having eyes in the air above an incident will enhance the awareness of the commander on the ground, to ensure his officers' safety and the public's safety," McDaniel says today. "You can't literally surround a building or a house every time. Having that drone up in the air above it can enhance safety for law enforcement." The device would also help in non-crime situations, McDaniel says, such as tracking down hikers who have lost their way in nearby Sam Houston National Forest. "People get lost in that forest every year," McDaniel says.

"It would certainly be more effective to put that UAV up as opposed to sending 30 or 40 search-and-rescue personnel to walk it."

Many First Responders Could Benefit

It's not just police departments that see big potential in unmanned drones. Fire departments and other emergency response teams could use them to help pinpoint the source of a building fire or, say, map a hazmat spill. The federal Department of Agriculture uses a drone to monitor experimental crops in Georgia and Alabama; state agriculture departments could no doubt find plenty of similar uses. Documents disclosed by a Freedom of Information Act request this summer from the Electronic Frontier Foundation showed that the federal government had approved drones for 18 public entities around the country, including police departments in Seattle, Miami-Dade, Fla., and North Little Rock, Ark., as well as places like Ohio University and the city of Herington, Kan. Thanks to anticipated changes in federal aviation regulations, thousands of private and commercial drones could also take to the air by 2015. According to FAA estimates, more than 30,000 drones could fill the American skies by 2020. As University of Texas assistant professor Todd Humphreys, who has investigated the use of domestic drones, testified to Congress earlier this year, "The UAV revolution is coming."

Needless to say, privacy concerns are huge. Nothing says "Big Brother police state" quite like the idea of faceless surveillance drones flitting through the sky, tracking and video-taping civilians' every move. According to one recent national poll, while 44 percent of Americans support the use of drones by police forces, a large minority—36 percent—were opposed because of the potential for privacy invasion. Those fears are further stoked by comments like a recent statement from Alameda County, Calif., Sheriff Gregory Ahern, who said his department, which has filed for drone clearance from the

FAA, would use the vehicles to troll for marijuana farms and other forms of "proactive policing."

Surveillance Suspicions

"Our ultimate concern is that drones become a tool for pervasive, routine, suspicionless surveillance," says Jay Stanley, a senior policy analyst for the American Civil Liberties Union's (ACLU) Speech, Privacy and Technology Project. "We don't want to see them used for 24/7 tracking of vehicles or individuals, and over towns or cities or neighborhoods. We don't want to see them used for individual suspicion. We don't want them to be used in ways that are invasive."

At the federal level, the ACLU has recommended that government use of drones be banned except in very specific cases.

Law enforcement officials say that's not their intention, and they couldn't use drones that way even if they wanted to. "We did not obtain this for the purpose of surveillance," says McDaniel. "Our ShadowHawk's maximum aloft time is only two hours and 20 minutes, and you would never fly it for that length of time to begin with." FAA regulations prohibit drones from flying higher than 400 feet, and they require that drones remain in line of sight of the user. In other words, says McDaniel, if a drone's around, you'll know it. "It's not like its 30,000 feet up in the air and you can't see it and you can't hear it. It's going to be visible to the naked eye, and you're certainly going to hear it."

Laws Should Preempt Problems

Current drone technology may not lend itself to stealth surveillance, but that's why privacy legislation should be passed now, before it becomes a problem, say advocates. "While drones are new and novel and everybody's worried about the privacy issue," says Stanley, "we need to put in place some far-seeing rules and protections that will cover every possible evolution of this technology." . . .

In August, the International Association of Chiefs of Police adopted guidelines for the use of unmanned aircraft. The guidelines call for transparency in how the vehicles are used, and say that any images captured by aerial drones and retained by police should be open to the public. In cases where drones might collect evidence of criminal wrongdoing, or if they will intrude on reasonable expectations of privacy, guidelines suggest police should obtain a prior search warrant. Those instructions aren't binding, but they're a good start, privacy advocates say.

At the federal level, the ACLU has recommended that government use of drones be banned except in very specific cases. One piece of legislation has been introduced in Congress by Republican Sen. Rand Paul of Kentucky, which would ban domestic governmental drone use except in patrolling the border or in high-risk security situations. The bill currently lacks bipartisan support. While the ACLU says the bill isn't perfect, its legislative counsel Chris Calabrese says the bill is "starting in the right place, and we're going to work with him as he moves forward."

Drone Spoofing and Hacking

In addition to questions about privacy, another concern is drones' security. First, there's the immediate worry that comes from allowing individually operated aircraft in domestic airspace, particularly in a post-9/11 world. That concern was borne out last year, when a man in Massachusetts was thwarted after attempting to equip several drones with C4 explosives and fly them into the Capitol and Pentagon. Second, civilian drones can be hacked, or "spoofed," by a counterfeit GPS signal. (Unlike military GPS signals, civilian signals are not encrypted.) The spoofed drone thinks it's in a different place, allowing the hacker to take rudimentary control of it. In a demonstration in June, the University of Texas' Humphreys led a team of researchers who successfully hacked into one drone's navigation system.

There's no question that unmanned aerial vehicles could forever change crime fighting, disaster response and a host of other functions.

Regulating this type of vehicle typically would fall under the purview of Homeland Security, but that department has so far declined to regulate the UAV industry. That's a major problem, says Texas Rep. Michael McCaul, who chairs the House Subcommittee on Oversight, Investigations and Management. "I find this to be a bit of a 'nobody's minding the store' type scenario," McCaul says. "No federal agency's willing to step up to the plate, and when you have the [Government Accountability Office] saying the DHS needs to do it, I tend to agree with them." Without regulation at the federal level, security oversight could fall to individual states.

For his part, Humphreys says he's not overly worried about drone security. Spoofing a UAV requires a high level of expertise and very expensive software. But as with the privacy issues, it's an issue that almost certainly will be exacerbated as technology advances. "What my nightmare scenario would be," he says, "is looking forward three or four years, where we have now adopted the UAVs into the national airspace without addressing this problem. Now the problem is scaling up, so that we have more heavy UAVs, more capable UAVs and yet this particular vulnerability isn't addressed."

There's no question that unmanned aerial vehicles could forever change crime fighting, disaster response and a host of other functions. Given the push from the federal government, it seems inevitable that drones will increasingly be a part of police assets around the country. But it's important to address concerns over privacy and security now, says Humphreys. "Let's let it go ahead," he says. "But let's be vigilant."

Drones Can Help Improve Public Safety

Colin Wood

Colin Wood has been writing for Government Technology *and* Emergency Management *magazines since 2010.*

While drones have been deployed in many military actions, domestic drone deployment in the United States faces opposition on several fronts. Many in the public view drones as overly invasive or machines of war, as demonstrated by the legislative acts of many states, capped off by Seattle's recent decision to scrap the police department's drone program.

But hobbyists and many in the public safety community argue that privacy concerns over drones may be keeping the public from seeing the true potential the unmanned aircraft could offer, especially in emergency management and response.

Law enforcement could use drones to gain better situational awareness and keep officers and civilians safe during dangerous operations like drug busts or hostage situations. Firefighters could use them to scout wildfires, or identify hidden hot spots in structure fires. Rescue teams could save trapped or missing people in areas that helicopters can't reach. In the right hands, drones could make the public safer.

For hobbyists, there are virtually no obstacles to flying a small, unmanned aircraft. A beginner drone costs a few hundred dollars, and the Federal Aviation Administration (FAA) allows toy drones to go essentially unregulated. But if a drone is used as a tool, whether for fire scouting or to bring water to a stranded hiker, then the drone is no longer a toy and requires a certificate of authorization. There's a lot of paperwork and months of waiting in store for any public safety agency seeking to use a drone legally. But this will soon change, according to Don Shinnamon, a former police chief who sat on the first rule-making committee for drones.

If a public safety agency has between $40,000 and $100,000 to spend on drone technology, they can get a turn-key system that works well.

"As a pilot of manned aircraft," Shinnamon said, "I don't necessarily want to be dodging a hundred unmanned aircraft that are flying around. So I support the notion that the integration of unmanned aircraft has to go slowly so we can guarantee the safety of the national airspace." While Shinnamon supports conservative drone legislation for safety purposes, he is also a major proponent of increased domestic drone use. He drafted a provision of the FAA Modernization and Reform Act of 2012 that will make it simpler for public safety agencies to get authorized.

Law Enforcement Looks to Cut Costs

With fewer regulations keeping law enforcement agencies from using drones, Shinnamon expects the technology will become a more viable option, especially given their potential to enhance public safety. "We are a tradition-bound profession," Shinnamon said, referring to those in law enforcement who don't support the use of drones, "but the economy has forced us to look for better ways to provide the same levels of service or more economical ways of providing a higher level of service. The technology has proven it can save the lives of troops on the ground in combat zones. And that same technology can provide a much higher level of safety for police officers and firefighters doing dangerous things here in our country."

But even those public safety leaders interested in reaping the benefits of drones don't necessarily have the knowledge, funding or time to research the technology. That's where hobbyists come in.

Hobbyists Help Sell Drone Idea

If a public safety agency has between $40,000 and $100,000 to spend on drone technology, they can get a turn-key system that works well, according to Oregon-based hobbyists Patrick Sherman and Brian Zvaigzne. Calling themselves the Roswell Flight Test Crew, the two are showing agencies in their region what drones can accomplish at a modest cost.

The team has worked with fire and rescue agencies in Portland, Ore.; Tualatin Valley, Ore.; Clackamas, Ore.; and Longview, Wash. Sherman reports that their level of involvement has ranged from preliminary talks to field demonstrations, and they've encountered wide variations in officials' openness to the potential of drones.

Commercial drones on the market today are much easier to control than those available just a few years ago.

"We've had some firefighters who've been just enthralled with the idea of this technology," he explained, but others staunchly defend their agency's current operations, questioning what value the unmanned craft would bring. "I'm not saying there's anything wrong with the way they do things. I think this can be an enhancement," Sherman said.

According to Sherman, drones made by hobbyists like the Roswell Flight Test Crew work as well as the big-name turn-key drone systems sold by commercial vendors, but cost about 95 percent less. But drones require maintenance, system integration and someone has to know how to fly them.

Unmanned Civil Air Patrol

Just as the Civil Air Patrol employs volunteer pilots to support operations of the U.S. Air Force, there are drone hobbyists around the country who might consider joining an unmanned civil air patrol, he suggests. "There's a long tradition of amateur radio operators helping out in emergencies," Sherman said, adding that until drone technology becomes more broadly used, drone hobbyists, similarly, could fill this vital role.

Commercial drones on the market today are much easier to control than those available just a few years ago. If a drone pilot takes his hands off the controls, GPS and altitude positioning allow the aircraft to simply hover in place until the pilot is ready to continue. This technological progress is thanks to engineers and researchers like Mary "Missy" Cummings, an associate professor at MIT who focuses much of her research on drone control architectures.

According to Cummings, a major reason drones have gotten cheaper in the last few years is that manufacturers have cut corners on things like user interface. "Unfortunately the big barrier to UAVs [Unmanned Aerial Vehicles] being successful in the commercial marketplace is that they're going to have to be as safe as commercial aircraft," she said. "Companies are going to have to start taking safety, efficiency, well designed interfaces, the reduction of human error, they're going to have to start taking that stuff seriously."

Cummings said although she liked the idea of an unmanned civil air patrol, she noted that there are several major barriers to implementation, including collision avoidance, command and control support and coordination.

Asset Management

Consider, she said, a major earthquake in California. "Like in a lot of cases where you have a community grass-roots effort, you need somebody who can actually manage this and now we're not talking about just managing people and rescuers, we're managing all the data that's going out to support rescuers." So while it's a good idea, she said, the program would need structure to make it work.

Regardless of whether a grass-roots effort can impact public safety in an emergency, drones can augment operations in ways that no other technology can, Cummings said. "These automated systems can exceed human abilities and take over in the times when we can't do something because of our physical limitations, and I think that is what we're going to start seeing in the future," she said. "You don't want to send a manned helicopter into a burning area to pick up, let's say, some firefighters that were pinned in by some out of control fire. You wouldn't want to risk a human life to do that, but you would easily send in a helicopter to do that."

Cummings thinks that it is just these kinds of emergency response scenarios that might help change public perceptions about drone use. "We're going to have the next Hurricane Katrina, the next Hurricane Sandy," she explained. "We're going to start seeing unmanned vehicles bringing in badly needed supplies and . . . I think as soon as we do that, it's going to be amazing the change we see in people. People just see UAVs as bad. I think there's a change coming."

Drones Are Vital for US Border Security

Perla Trevizo

Perla Trevizo is a staff writer for the Arizona Daily Star *newspaper.*

B order security is the first step of the proposed immigration reform bill—and some lawmakers see 24/7 surveillance as a key to stopping illegal crossers.

Ten drones already fly along the U.S. southern and northern borders. But U.S. Customs and Border Protection [CBP] has not been able to fully use them, partly because of Federal Aviation Administration restrictions and partly because of a lack of money to operate them, said Randolph Alles, assistant commander of the Office of Air and Marine, which supervises the drones.

After nearly eight years of operating drones along the border, Alles said the agency is now reaping the benefits, but the program is still not where he wants it to be.

"Looking backward, it probably would have been better if we were able to bring them on slower," he said.

The most commonly used drone, the Predator B, can fly about 20 hours without having to refuel, compared with a helicopter's average flight time of just over two hours. With new technology such as VADER, Alles said the agency is getting more use out of the aircraft than before.

VADER, which stands for Vehicle and Dismount Exploitation Radar, was developed for the war in Afghanistan. It lets agents track activity in real time and distinguishes humans from animals from an altitude of 25,000 feet. Last year, CBP borrowed the radar from the military to test it in Arizona.

U.S. Sen. John McCain is among VADER's supporters.

A total of 10 drones fly now [for border control]—five days a week, 16 hours a day out of Sierra Vista [Arizona] and five days a week, 10 hours a day out of the locations in Texas, Florida and North Dakota.

"It seems to me that's an incredible technology tool," McCain told Alles during a congressional hearing in April [2013]. "Don't you believe that VADER plus drones could be absolute vital tools in attaining effective control of our border?"

As lawmakers started to debate the immigration bill last week [June 2013], McCain said the government needed to use more technology such as drones and VADER to increase border security.

Boosting Drone Effectiveness

Alles would not comment on possible requirements of the immigration bill, saying his immediate goal is to get better use out of the drones he has by training more personnel, flying the dones longer and attaching better surveillance equipment to the aircraft.

A total of 10 drones fly now—five days a week, 16 hours a day out of Sierra Vista and five days a week, 10 hours a day out of the locations in Texas, Florida and North Dakota.

Alles' long-term goal is to fly drones seven days a week, 16 hours a day—"we are not there yet," he said.

CBP's original plan was to purchase 24 unmanned aircraft, but Alles said he doesn't have the money to buy more—and even if he did, he doesn't have enough money to operate them all.

The agency spends $32 million to $34 million to operate and maintain the 10 aircraft a year. That includes expenses related to ground-control stations, repairs, satellite communication and engineering support. The total cost of the program has been estimated at several hundred million dollars.

In fiscal year 2010, CBP had to transfer $25 million from other programs to address operations and maintenance funding shortfalls.

Since the program's inception, critics have questioned if the $18 million cost for each fully equipped aircraft is the best use of taxpayer money.

"Desired Capability"

If CBP were flying seven drones—the number the agency had at the time of a 2012 report by Homeland Security's inspector general—it would need to fly them 13,328 flight hours annually to reach its "desired capability."

At a per-hour flight cost of $3,234, that would require nearly $62 million per year—about 12 percent of the entire operations, maintenance, and procurement budget for CBP's Air and Marine branch.

Given the operational cost of the Predator B, the amount of drugs and people the drones help seize is not impressive, said Adam Isacson, a regional security policy expert for the Washington Office on Latin America, an organization that studies the effects of U.S. policies on Latin America.

Nationwide, drones have helped seize more than $650 million worth of drugs.

The four drones based in Sierra Vista—which fly mostly along the Southwest border but can be shifted to other areas as needed—have flown nearly 12,000 hours and helped seize 82,000 pounds of marijuana since fiscal 2006. CBP didn't provide the number of apprehensions.

From fiscal years 2008 through last month, Border Patrol agents along the Southwest border seized more than 13 million pounds of marijuana.

Nationwide, drones have helped seize more than $650 million worth of drugs, "which basically pays for the program by itself," Alles said.

The unmanned aircraft are also used during floods and hurricanes, he said, although 95 percent of their missions are along the borders.

VADER Sees All

VADER is helping, too. The radar can detect about 11 people an hour, Alles said, more than any other detection tools in the system, including fixed towers or other aircraft.

Isacson said drones and radars like VADER, though expensive, will help CBP see more of what's going on at the border, which is good.

But he questions if the agency will have the personnel needed to catch everything detected on the nearly 2,000-mile stretch of the southern border.

The Center for Investigative Reporting and the *Los Angeles Times* reported that Border Patrol agents last year apprehended fewer than half of the people VADER spotted crossing into a stretch of Southern Arizona.

Among the limitations, the internal reports revealed that Border Patrol agents often are not available to respond because of rugged terrain or other assignments, the Center for Investigative Reporting found.

Alles said the internal report was misused and doesn't reflect apprehensions in the zone where the radar was used. CBP is getting two of the $5 million VADER systems and plans to deploy at least one in Arizona in about a year. At the recent Congressional hearing he told McCain the goal was to have six radars.

Whatever shape comprehensive immigration reform takes in the end, Isacson said, it's not likely to pass without requiring the use of more drones.

"Putting more drones and technology on the border is an easy way to convince more conservative members of Congress to vote for this," he said. "It feels it's inevitable."

Law Enforcement Drones Pose Multiple Dangers

Glenn Greenwald

Glenn Greenwald is an American journalist and lawyer best known for exposing the National Security Agency's (NSA) mass surveillance programs based on classified information leaked by former intelligence contractor Edward Snowden.

The use of drones by domestic US law enforcement agencies is growing rapidly, both in terms of numbers and types of usage. As a result, civil liberties and privacy groups led by the ACLU [American Civil Liberties Union]—while accepting that domestic drones are inevitable—have been devoting increasing efforts to publicizing their unique dangers and agitating for statutory limits. These efforts are being impeded by those who mock the idea that domestic drones pose unique dangers (often the same people who mock concern over their usage on foreign soil). This dismissive posture is grounded not only in soft authoritarianism (a religious-type faith in the Goodness of US political leaders and state power generally) but also ignorance over current drone capabilities, the ways drones are now being developed and marketed for domestic use, and the activities of the increasingly powerful domestic drone lobby. So it's quite worthwhile to lay out the key under-discussed facts shaping this issue.

I'm going to focus here most on domestic surveillance drones, but I want to say a few words about weaponized drones. The belief that weaponized drones won't be used on US soil is patently irrational. Of course they will be. It's not just likely but inevitable. Police departments are already speaking openly about how their drones "could be equipped to carry nonlethal weapons such as Tasers or a bean-bag gun." The drone industry has already developed and is now aggressively marketing precisely such weaponized drones for domestic law enforcement use. It likely won't be in the form that has received the most media attention: the type of large Predator or Reaper drones that shoot Hellfire missiles which destroy homes and cars in Pakistan, Yemen, Somalia, Afghanistan and multiple other countries aimed at Muslims (although US law enforcement agencies already possess Predator drones and have used them over US soil for surveillance).

The handful of genuinely positive uses from drones will be endlessly touted to distract attention away from the dangers they pose.

Cheap and Agile Weaponized Drones

Instead, as I detailed in a 2012 examination of the drone industry's own promotional materials and reports to their shareholders, domestic weaponized drones will be much smaller and cheaper, as well as more agile—but just as lethal. The nation's leading manufacturer of small "unmanned aircraft systems" (UAS), used both for surveillance and attack purposes, is AeroVironment, Inc. (AV). Its 2011 Annual Report filed with the SEC [Securities Exchange Commission] repeatedly emphasizes that its business strategy depends upon expanding its market from foreign wars to domestic usage including law enforcement:

> "As we explore opportunities to develop new markets for our small UAS, such as border surveillance, law enforcement, first response and infrastructure monitoring, we expect further growth through the introduction of UAS technology to non-military applications once rules are established for their safe and effective operation in each country's national airspace."

AV's annual report added: "Initial likely non-military users of small UAS include public safety organizations such as law enforcement agencies. . . ." These domestic marketing efforts are intensifying with the perception that US spending on foreign wars will decrease. As a February, 2013 CBS News report noted, focusing on AV's surveillance drones:

> "Now, drones are headed off the battlefield. They're already coming your way."

> "AeroVironment (AV), the California company that sells the military something like 85 percent of its fleet, is marketing them now to public safety agencies."

Like many drone manufacturers, AV is now focused on drone products—such as the "Qube"—that are so small that they can be "transported in the trunk of a police vehicle or carried in a backpack" and assembled and deployed within a matter of minutes. One news report AV touts is headlined "Drone technology could be coming to a Police Department near you," which focuses on the Qube.

"The Ultimate Assassin Bug"

But another article prominently touted on AV's website describes the tiny UAS product dubbed the "Switchblade," which, says the article, is "the leading edge of what is likely to be the broader, even wholesale, weaponization of unmanned systems." The article creepily hails the Switchblade drone as "*the ultimate assassin bug*." That's because, as I wrote back in 2011, "it is controlled by the operator at the scene, and it worms its way around buildings and into small areas, sending its surveillance imagery to an i-Pad held by the operator, who can then direct the Switchblade to lunge toward and kill the target (hence the name) by exploding in his face." AV's website right now proudly touts a February, 2013 *Defense News* article describing how much the US Army loves the "Switchblade" and how it is preparing to purchase more. *Time* magazine heralded this tiny drone weapon as "one of the best inventions of 2012," gushing: "the Switchblade drone can be carried into battle in a backpack. It's a kamikaze: the person controlling it uses a real-time video feed from the drone to crash it into a precise target—say, a sniper. Its tiny warhead detonates on impact."

What possible reason could someone identify as to why these small, portable weaponized UAS products will not imminently be used by federal, state and local law enforcement agencies in the US? They're designed to protect their users in dangerous situations and to enable a target to be more easily killed. Police agencies and the increasingly powerful drone industry will tout their utility in capturing and killing dangerous criminals and their ability to keep officers safe, and media reports will do the same. The handful of genuinely positive uses from drones will be endlessly touted to distract attention away from the dangers they pose.

Unmanned aircraft carrying cameras raise the prospect of a significant new avenue for the surveillance of American life.

The Militarization of Law Enforcement

One has to be incredibly naïve to think that these "assassin bugs" and other lethal drone products will not be widely used on US soil by an already para-militarized domestic police force. As Radley Balko's forthcoming book *Rise of the Warrior Cop* details, the primary trend in US law enforcement is what its title describes as "The Militarization of America's Police Forces." The history of domestic law enforcement particularly after 9/11 has been the importation of military techniques and weapons into domestic policing. It would be shocking if these weapons were not imminently used by domestic law enforcement agencies.

In contrast to weaponized drones, even the most naïve among us do not doubt the imminent proliferation of domestic surveillance drones. With little debate, they have already arrived. As the ACLU put it in their recent report: "US law enforcement is greatly expanding its use of domestic drones for surveillance." An *LA Times* article from last month [February 2013] reported that "federal authorities have stepped up efforts to license surveillance drones for law enforcement and other uses in US airspace" and that "the Federal Aviation Administration said Friday it had issued 1,428 permits to domestic drone operators since 2007, far more than were previously known." Moreover, the agency "has estimated 10,000 drones could be aloft five years later" and "local and state law enforcement agencies are expected to be among the largest customers."

"The Gorgon Stare"

Concerns about the proliferation of domestic surveillance drones are typically dismissed with the claim that they do nothing more than police helicopters and satellites already do. Such claims are completely misinformed. As the ACLU's 2011 comprehensive report on domestic drones explained: "Unmanned aircraft carrying cameras raise the prospect of a significant new avenue for the surveillance of American life."

Multiple attributes of surveillance drones make them uniquely threatening. Because they are so cheap and getting cheaper, huge numbers of them can be deployed to create ubiquitous surveillance in a way that helicopters or satellites never could. How this works can already been seen in Afghanistan, where the US military has dubbed its drone surveillance system "the Gorgon Stare," named after the "mythical Greek creature whose unblinking eyes turned to stone those who beheld them." That drone surveillance system is "able to scan an area the size of a small town" and "the most sophisticated robotics use artificial intelligence that [can] seek out and record certain kinds of suspicious activity." Boasted one US General: "Gorgon Stare will be looking at a whole city, so there will be no way for the adversary to know what we're looking at, and *we can see everything.*"

In sum, surveillance drones enable a pervasive, stealth and constantly hovering Surveillance State that is now well beyond the technological and financial abilities of law enforcement agencies.

Drones and the Surveillance State

The NSA [National Security Agency] already maintains ubiquitous surveillance of electronic communications, but the Surveillance State faces serious limits on its ability to replicate that for physical surveillance. Drones easily overcome those barriers. As the ACLU report put it:

> "But manned aircraft are expensive to purchase, operate and maintain, and this expense has always imposed a natural limit on the government's aerial surveillance capability. Now that surveillance can be carried out by unmanned aircraft, this natural limit is eroding. The prospect of cheap, small, portable flying video surveillance machines threatens to eradicate existing practical limits on aerial monitoring and allow for pervasive surveillance, police fishing expeditions, and abusive use of these tools in a way that could eventually eliminate the privacy Americans have traditionally enjoyed in their movements and activities."

I've spoken previously about why a ubiquitous Surveillance State ushers in unique and deeply harmful effects on human behavior and a nation's political culture and won't repeat that here. . . . Suffice to say, as the ACLU explains in its domestic drone report: "routine aerial surveillance would profoundly change the character of public life in America" because *only* drone technology enables such omnipresent physical surveillance.

Beyond that, the tiny size of surveillance drones enables them to reach places that helicopters obviously cannot, and to do so without detection. They can remain in the sky, hovering over a single place, for up to 20 hours, a duration that is always increasing—obviously far more than manned helicopters can achieve. As AV's own report put it, their hovering capability also means they can surveil a single spot for much longer than many military satellites, most of which move with the earth's rotation (the few satellites that remain fixed "operate nearly 25,000 miles from the surface of the earth, therefore limiting the bandwidth they can provide and requiring relatively larger, higher power ground stations"). In sum, surveillance drones enable a pervasive, stealth and constantly hovering Surveillance State that is now well beyond the technological and financial abilities of law enforcement agencies.

Only the most authoritarian among us will be incapable of understanding the multiple dangers posed by a domestic drone regime.

The Drone Lobby Is Powerful

One significant reason why this proliferation of domestic drones has become so likely is the emergence of a powerful drone lobby. I detailed some of how that lobby is functioning here, so will simply note this passage from a recent report from the ACLU of Iowa on its attempts to persuade legislators to enact statutory limits on the use of domestic drones:

> "Drones have their own trade group, the Association for Unmanned Aerial Systems International, which includes some of the nation's leading aerospace companies. And Congress now has 'drone caucuses' in both the Senate and House."

[Progressive blogger] Howie Klein has been one of the few people focusing on the massive amounts of money from the drone industry now flowing into the coffers of key Congressional members from both parties in this "drone caucus." Suffice to say, there is an enormous profit to be made from exploiting the domestic drone market, and as usual, that factor is thus far driving the (basically nonexistent) political response to these threats.

What is most often ignored by drone proponents, or those who scoff at anti-drone activism, are the unique features of drones: the way they enable more warfare, more aggression, and more surveillance. Drones make war more likely precisely because they entail so little risk to the war-making country. Similarly, while the propensity of drones to kill innocent people receives the bulk of media attention, the way in which drones psychologically terrorize the population—simply by constantly hovering over them: unseen but heard—is usually ignored, because it's not happening in the US, so few people care. It remains to be seen how Americans will react to drones constantly hovering over their homes and their childrens' schools, though by that point, their presence will be so institutionalized that it will likely be too late to stop.

The Dangers of a Domestic Drone Regime

Notably, this may be one area where an actual bipartisan/ trans-partisan alliance can meaningfully emerge, as most advocates working on these issues with whom I've spoken say that libertarian-minded GOP state legislators have been as responsive as more left-wing Democratic ones in working to impose some limits. One bill now pending in Congress would prohibit the use of surveillance drones on US soil in the absence of a specific search warrant, and has bipartisan support.

Only the most authoritarian among us will be incapable of understanding the multiple dangers posed by a domestic drone regime (particularly when their party is in control of the government and they are incapable of perceiving threats from increased state police power). But the proliferation of domestic drones affords a real opportunity to forge an enduring coalition in defense of core privacy and other rights that transcends partisan allegiance, by working toward meaningful limits on their use. Making people aware of exactly what these unique threats are from a domestic drone regime is the key first step in constructing that coalition.

Law Enforcement Drones Spur Public Backlash

Nadia Prupis

Nadia Prupis is a staff writer for Common Dreams, *a news and analysis website for the progressive community.*

Police departments in the U.S. are increasingly considering the use of drones as a law enforcement tool, even as civil rights groups and media turn up scrutiny of police militarization in the wake of brutal crackdowns on anti-brutality protesters in Ferguson, Missouri and other cities.

The *Baltimore Sun* reported on Sunday [August 24, 2014] that agencies in several Maryland counties are considering testing drones, or unmanned aerial vehicles (UAVs), for intelligence gathering and "high-risk tactical raids." That news comes less than a week after anti-war activists in California protested against "mission creep" by the Los Angeles Police Department (LAPD) which recently acquired several of their own drones. Indiana police departments also recently announced their plan to pursue adding drones to their weapons arsenal. In a letter to LA Mayor Eric Garcetti, Drone-Free LA spokesperson Hamid Kahn expressed "deep concerns about the recent 'gifting' of two Draganflyer X Drones" by the Seattle Police Department [SPD] to the LAPD. "We believe the acquisition of drones signifies a giant step forward in the militarization of local law enforcement that is normalizing continued surveillance and violations of human rights of our communities," Kahn wrote.

The SPD originally purchased the unmanned aerial vehicles using a federal grant called the Urban Areas Security

Initiative—a common example of the effects of the government's pervasive, $34-billion militarization program that enables domestic police departments to acquire and trade tools and weapons intended for warfare. In a June press conference, LAPD chief Charlie Beck said drones would be useful in "standoffs, perimeters, suspects hiding," and defended the department's acquisition of the UAVs by stating, "When retailers start talking about using them to deliver packages, we would be silly not to at least have a discussion of whether we want to use them in law enforcement."

A lot of what can be done with this equipment is very much questionable, as far as adherence to the Fourth Amendment.

Critics Sound the Alarm

But while many police departments claim that they would use the vehicles strictly for high-risk scenarios, critics have sounded the alarm over the risks of drone use, particularly by entities they say are as historically oppressive as American law enforcement agencies.

Tara Tabassi, national organizer with the War Resisters League, told *Common Dreams* that with the "current nationwide public outcry against police militarization, it is the many invisible methods of domestic warfare, such as the use of drones by police departments, that must be a major focus. . . . Warfare indeed knows no borders, nor does the US government's lack of transparency and accountability as they choose to protect the identities and crimes of drone operators over the civil liberties and human rights of unarmed populations across the globe."

Police militarization and violent police responses to peaceful protests have faced increased scrutiny in recent weeks after activists and reporters in Ferguson were tear gassed and shot at while demanding justice for Michael Brown, the unarmed teenager who was shot to death by a police officer earlier this month. "A lot of what can be done with this equipment is very much questionable, as far as adherence to the Fourth Amendment," Nathan Sheard, a campaign organizer with anti-war group CodePink, told *Common Dreams*. "The fact that it's being paid for by Department of Homeland Security shows a very obvious connection with militarization. When police departments start to be armed . . . as military forces, rather than protecting and serving, they start occupying and oppressing."

Fourth Amendment Worries

In California, Kahn pointed to the LAPD's history of "lies, brutality, and violence against communities," and said that the department is "incapable of creating any policy that would protect our human and civil rights."

Sheard also noted "the very real possibility of installing infrared cameras" on UAVs, models of which have already appeared in the U.S.

The risks are "beyond what's just visible to the eye," Sheard said. "These are cameras that would pick up heat signals rather than video. How does that play into the Fourth Amendment protections against search and seizure?"

David Rocah, senior staff attorney with the ACLU of Maryland, told *WJZ* that drones pose an inherent risk to the right to privacy. "That is completely incompatible with a free society and I think poses real dangers and is a real possibility unless we act to prevent it," Rocah said.

Regulation of drone technology is a concern as well. Claims from police departments that the UAVs would be used transparently and "would not sacrifice public trust," as LAPD spokesperson Bruce Borhian told *KNX*, are not enough, Sheard said.

The Fox Guarding the Henhouse?

"Who is monitoring [the police]?" Sheard told *Common Dreams*. "Who's holding them accountable? What ability do citizens have to view that information? Where do those recordings go? There are just too many questions." He noted a successful CodePink campaign to end the use of drones by a department in Washington state that simply resulted in the vehicles being traded to an agency in California. "The equipment just changed hands," Sheard said.

"Now is the time to stop the engine of surveillance technology and state repression," Tabassi told *Common Dreams*. "By continuing to build across all communities mobilizing against police militarization, we can effectively resist the solidifying relationship between the Pentagon and police departments, demanding an end to all drones, and militarization more broadly."

Pending Senate approval, the presence of drones in US airspace is projected to increase by 10,000 in 2015, Tabassi said. Although the use of drones by police departments is still in relative infancy, waiting on testing and Federal Aviation Administration rules, more than 500 agencies were approved to use them in the last year alone.

Drones Are Ineffective for Border Patrol

Brian Bennett

Brian Bennett covers homeland security and immigration for the Los Angeles Times *newspaper.*

Drones patrolling the U.S. border are poorly managed and ineffective at stopping illegal immigration, and the government should abandon a $400-million plan to expand their use, according to an internal watchdog report released Tuesday [January 6, 2015].

The 8-year-old drone program has cost more than expected, according to a report by the Department of Homeland Security's inspector general, John Roth.

Rather than spend more on drones, the department should "put those funds to better use," Roth recommended. He described the Predator B drones flown along the border by U.S. Customs and Border Protection as "dubious achievers."

"Notwithstanding the significant investment, we see no evidence that the drones contribute to a more secure border, and there is no reason to invest additional taxpayer funds at this time," Roth said in a statement.

The audit concluded that Customs and Border Protection could better use the funds on manned aircraft and ground surveillance technology.

The drones were designed to fly over the border to spot smugglers and illegal border crossers. But auditors found that 78% of the time that agents had planned to use the craft, they were grounded because of bad weather, budget constraints or maintenance problems.

Drones Contribute Little to Arrests

Even when aloft, auditors found, the drones contributed little. Three drones flying around the Tucson area helped apprehend about 2,200 people illegally crossing the border in 2013, fewer than 2% of the 120,939 apprehended that year in the area.

Border Patrol supervisors had planned on using drones to inspect ground-sensor alerts. But a drone was used in that scenario only six times in 2013.

Time after time, we see the practical realities of these systems don't live up to the hype.

Auditors found that officials underestimated the cost of the drones by leaving out operating costs such as pilot salaries, equipment and overhead. Adding such items increased the flying cost nearly fivefold, to $12,255 per hour.

"It really doesn't feel like [Customs and Border Protection] has a good handle on how it is using its drones, how much it costs to operate the drones, where that money is coming from or whether it is meeting any of its performance metrics," said Jennifer Lynch, a lawyer for the Electronic Frontier Foundation, a San Francisco-based privacy and digital rights group.

The report's conclusions will make it harder for officials to justify further investment in the border surveillance drones, especially at a time when Homeland Security's budget is at the center of the battle over President [Barack] Obama's program to give work permits to millions of immigrants in the country illegally. Each Predator B system costs about $20 million.

No Silver Bullet

"People think these kinds of surveillance technologies will be a silver bullet," said Jay Stanley, a privacy expert at the American Civil Liberties Union. "Time after time, we see the practical realities of these systems don't live up to the hype."

Customs and Border Protection, which is part of Homeland Security, operates the fleet of nine long-range Predator B drones from bases in Arizona, Texas and North Dakota.

The agency purchased 11 drones, but one crashed in Arizona in 2006 and another fell into the Pacific Ocean off San Diego after a mechanical failure last year.

Agency officials said in response to the audit that they had no plans to expand the fleet aside from replacing the Predator that crashed last year. The agency is authorized to spend an additional $433 million to buy up to 14 more drones.

The drones—unarmed versions of the MQ-9 Reaper drone flown by the Air Force to hunt targets in Pakistan, Somalia and elsewhere—fly the vast majority of their missions in narrowly defined sections of the Southwest border, the audit found.

They spent most of their time along 100 miles of border in Arizona near Tucson and 70 miles of border in Texas.

Better Measures of Effectiveness Are Needed

Rep. Henry Cuellar (D-Texas) has promoted the use of drones along the border but believes the agency should improve how it measures their effectiveness.

Homeland Security "can't prove the program is effective because they don't have the right measures," Cuellar said in an interview. "The technology is good, but how you implement and use it—that is another question."

The audit also said that drones had been flown to help the FBI [Federal Bureau of Investigation], the Texas Department of Public Safety and the Minnesota Department of Natural Resources.

Such missions have long frustrated Border Patrol agents, who complain that drones and other aircraft aren't available when they need them, said Shawn Moran, vice president of the Border Patrol agents' union.

"We saw the drones were being lent out to many entities for nonborder-related operations and we said, 'These drones, if they belong to [Customs and Border Protection], should be used to support [its] operations primarily,'" Moran said.

Demand for Domestic Drones Fuels the Military-Industrial Complex

Tom Barry

Tom Barry is cofounder of the Center for International Policy, a nonprofit public policy research and advocacy think tank in Washington, DC. Barry directs the Center's TransBorder Project whose goal is to foster policy alternatives and improve understanding of transborder issues such as immigration, homeland security, border security, and the national security complex.

The continuing rise of Predator drones at home has been fueled by the bizarre merger of military influence in domestic affairs and the key role of border hawks in the politics of immigration reform. DHS's [Department of Homeland Security] early decision to tap generals involved in the military's own controversial overseas drone program to shape and direct the domestic drone program points to the increasing merger of the post-9/11 homeland security/border security complex with the military-industrial complex.

Drone proliferation at home will likely increase from a multibillion-dollar spending surge to boost "border security" as a result of congressional proposals to reform immigration policy.

At home and abroad, drone proliferation has benefited from a broad bipartisan consensus about the purported success of the US military's foreign deployment of Predator drones in counterterrorism operations by the Pentagon and intelligence apparatus. Drone proliferation at home is closely linked to military and CIA enthusiasm for what are formally called unmanned aerial vehicles (UAVs), or simply unmanned systems.

Government reports [have] pointed to the complete absence of any cost-benefit evaluations and efficiency assessments of the DHS drone program.

DHS decided—with virtually no reviews or evaluations—to purchase unarmed versions of the Predator drones used abroad for "signature strikes" (targeted drone killing). The department, whose mission includes "border security," has also relied on military bases along the land border and coastal waters to host its own drone fleet.

Reports Contradict Effectiveness

Since DHS began acquiring Predators, along with Predator variants called Guardians, from General Atomics nine years ago, this domestic drone program has proved an abysmal failure—whether measured by its effectiveness in immigration enforcement, drug control, or counterterrorism. A series of reports by the General Accountability Office, Congressional Review Service, and the DHS Inspector General's Office have documented the paltry achievements, the alarming strategic confusion, and near-systemic logistical and technical shortcomings of the DHS drone program.

These government reports pointed to the complete absence of any cost-benefit evaluations and efficiency assessments of the DHS drone program.

Yet these official reviews failed to shed any light on the department's controversial decision to deploy only the hugely expensive military-grade Predator drones and to enter into sole-source contracts with General Atomics to provide, maintain, and even operate the federal government's domestic drone fleet.

Nor did they probe the decision by DHS to hire military men to run the domestic drone program, despite their total lack of experience in law enforcement, border control, drug control, and immigration enforcement. Instead, from the start, DHS brought in generals with a history of procurement and management of the military's killer drones to hunt down immigrants and illegal drugs with Predator drones.

The continuing rise of Predator drones at home has been fueled by the bizarre merger of military influence in domestic affairs and by the key role of border hawks in the politics of immigration reform. The decision early on by DHS to tap generals involved in the military's own controversial overseas drone program to shape and direct the domestic drone program points to the increasing merger of the post-9/11 homeland security/border security complex with the military-industrial complex.

Drones Feature in Immigration Reform

Congressional proponents of immigration reform have included repeated references to their commitment to provide dramatically increased aerial surveillance of the southwestern border by Department of Homeland Security drones.

Prominent immigration reform advocates such as Sen. Charles Schumer (D-NY) and Cong. Henry Cuellar (D-Texas) insist that "continuous" and "24 hours, seven days a week" drone surveillance is a fundamental condition of successful immigration reform. Yet these and other border drone advocates don't point to the achievements of the current DHS program. Rather, like Cuellar, they point to the purported success of the US military's antiterrorist drone program.

"We gotta have efficiencies, effectiveness, accountability on how they're used," he said. "But again, keep in mind, look at the history how they've been used extremely well in the military," said Cuellar, who cochairs the Congressional Caucus on Unmanned Systems, commonly known as the "Drone Caucus."

The [Office of Air and Marine] strategic plan calls for a fleet of two dozen drones by 2015—a goal that seemed unlikely to be reached given budget-cutting and the abysmal performance record of the OAM drones.

The DHS drone program is run by the Office of Air and Marine (OAM), a division of the Customs and Border Protection (CBP), which also includes the Office of the US Border Patrol.

Prior to 9/11 and DHS's creation, the Border Patrol and the US Customs Service (the legacy agency that became ICE), the various Border Patrol and US Customs sector offices mainly tapped their planes and boats to do what these agencies have traditionally done, namely apprehended unauthorized immigrants and seize illegal drugs. Under OAM, the actual operations remain largely the same, although now framed in a new security, counterterrorism context. According to CBP, the mission of OAM is "to detect, interdict, and prevent acts of terrorism and the unlawful movement of people, illegal drugs and other contraband towards or across the borders of the United States."

OAM boasts that it "is the most experienced operator of Unmanned Aircraft Systems in the Homeland Security mission set on the world stage."

OAM currently has a fleet of 10 Predator and Guardian drones manufactured by General Atomics. The OAM strategic plan calls for a fleet of two dozen drones by 2015—a goal that seemed unlikely to be reached given budget-cutting and the abysmal performance record of the OAM drones.

Questions Worth Asking

The first and signature initiative of the newly created OAM was to enter into a collaborative venture with General Atomics for unmanned Predator drones for border security operations—the first of which was deployed from Ft. Huachuca Army Base in Sierra Vista, Arizona shortly after the founding of OAM. In April 2006, this first CBP Predator crashed and was totaled in the Arizona desert due to a control error by the remote piloting team contracted from General Atomics.

Since 2005, when CBP deployed its first major drone, the UAV program of DHS has been the subject of mounting concern and criticisms from the government's own oversight and research agencies, including the Congressional Research Service, the Governmental Accountability Office, and the DHS's own Office of Inspector General.

In addition to the types of questions about worth and efficiency noted above, CBP/OAM has failed to adequately answer the following questions:

1. Why it so quickly decided that a drone fleet was necessary for border security?

2. Why it decided that the Predator UAV was the best fit?

3. Why it has continued the exclusive relationship with General Atomics despite the dubious accomplishment of these expensive military-developed drones?

Predator Drones Get Special Treatment

In November 2012, CBP did sign a sole-source contract with General Atomics Aeronautical Systems to provide maintenance and operating crews for its current contingent of UAVs and to purchase as many as 14 additional drones. But there was little hope that the money could be found until drones became a core component to the "border surge" advocated by Sen. Schumer earlier this year.

Whether at home or in South Asia, Predators get special treatment by the federal government, benefiting from sole-source, no-bid contracts. In October, DHS signed a new sole-source contract with General Atomics Aeronautical Systems. The $443.1 million five-year contract includes $237.7 million for the purchase of up to 14 additional Predators and Predator variants, and $205.4 million for operational costs and maintenance by General Atomics teams.

CBP insists that there is only one "responsible source" for its drone needs and that no other suppliers or servicers can satisfy agency requirements for these $18 million drones.

In a November 1 statement titled "Justification for Other than Full and Open Competition," DHS contends that General Atomics Aeronautical Systems Inc.'s (GA-ASI) knowledge of the production, operation, and maintenance of the MQ-9 [Predator] is so unique that a transition of OAM UAS equipment to a UAS other than the MQ-9 or support services to a company other than GA-ASI "would notably impact the CBP UAS program," including "appreciably impacting national security through decreased interdictions of contraband (e.g., illegal narcotics, undocumented immigrants)."

CHAPTER 4

Should Commercial Drone Use Be Allowed?

Chapter Preface

For decades, Americans have enjoyed the hobby of flying model airplanes and copters with little worry about regulations or licensing requirements. As long as remote-controlled aircraft weigh less than fifty-five pounds, fly below four hundred feet, avoid airports, stay within sight, and are not used for commercial purposes of any kind, the Federal Aviation Administration (FAA) does not regulate their use.

Those are the strictures that would-be commercial drone operators found themselves chaffing against as small, affordable consumer drones became widely available and demand spiked for their use in photography, agriculture, and other commercial interests.

But even as hobby drones soared in popularity over the past few years, their commercial use remained strictly illegal and many drone users were breaking the rules without even realizing it. The FAA has long defined "commercial use" so broadly that simply uploading amateur drone video to You-Tube—which an untold number of drone hobbyists have done—constitutes a violation that can draw fines of $10,000, and indeed has.

Meanwhile, a growing chorus of lobbyists from such diverse industries as construction, mining, film production, agriculture, energy, utilities, news media, real estate, and online retail began imploring the FAA to lift its ban on the commercial use of drones. In response, Congress gave the FAA a mandate to develop regulations for drone use and to open the nation's airspace to commercial drone traffic by September 30, 2015.

As it worked since 2012 to create the new rules, the FAA issued several hundred commercial drone operation permits on a case-by-case basis, primarily to law enforcement, universities, and agriculture groups, and it established a handful of sites around the country for commercial drone testing.

The agency has been roundly criticized for its slow pace in developing the guidelines and for missing several key progress benchmarks during the process, but a draft version of the long-awaited document was released for public comment in February 2015. As of this writing, it was unclear how heavily it might be revised or whether it would be enacted on schedule; some analysts think the rules are unlikely to be finalized before early 2017.

"Drones are an important technology for business, law enforcement, agriculture and more, but the lack of clear rules about small drones, the difference between commercial and a hobby drone, and how and where they can be used, is creating a serious threat to . . . safety," US senator Charles Schumer (D-NY) said in a press release after urging the FAA to expedite its rulemaking in the fall of 2014.[1]

FAA administrator Michael Huerta has defended his agency's progress, telling *Politico* that safety is exactly why the FAA has taken its time to get the drone issue right.

"There are proponents of unmanned aircraft, and they see huge potential of this technology—and for them, we can't move fast enough," Huerta said. "What they would like to see is free and open use of unmanned aircraft as soon as we can get there. On the other side," he added, "we have pilots—commercial pilots and general aviation pilots—who are very concerned that these are difficult to see, and they don't have a really good understanding of how they interact with other aircraft."[2]

1. Quoted in William Cole, "Drones Left Up in the Air," *Honolulu Star-Advertiser*, December 8, 2014.

2. Quoted in Jennifer Shutt, "FAA Administrator on the Future of Drones," *Politico*, November 30, 2014. http://www.politico.com/story/2014/11/drones-future-faa-michael -huerta-113214.html#ixzz3cu3H3ylQ.

If the FAA's rules are enacted as written in the February 2015 draft, drone users would have to take an airspace rules exam every two years and get an operator certificate, among other use criteria. (Those who fly model airplanes that meet existing guidelines would continue to be governed by them.)

The newly proposed rules would also effectively end the ban on commercial drones and allow them to fly at low altitudes within view of a ground-based pilot. Because that will essentially limit commercial drones to short-distance tasks, online retailers like Amazon who envisioned a shiny fleet of drones delivering packages to consumers' doorsteps remain out of luck, at least for now. Nevertheless, the proposed rules officially inaugurate the commercial drone era and represent a giant boon for the emerging drone economy.

The authors in this chapter explore the potential benefits and safety concerns of commercial drones and consider the question of whether commercial drone use should be allowed.

Commercial Drones Have Endless Potential

Rachel Janik and Mitchell Armentrout

Rachel Janik and Mitchell Armentrout wrote this viewpoint for the Medill News Service, a program of the Medill School of Journalism at Northwestern University in Evanston, Illinois.

The next time you feel the urge for fresh Mexican food, just look up. A taco-toting drone may be circling in the sky above you.

Researchers at the Darwin Aerospace laboratory in San Francisco have designed the Burrito Bomber, the world's first airborne Mexican food delivery system that would allow customers to have food parachuted right to their doorstep.

As fun as they may be to think about, such ideas aren't likely to be realized anytime soon. The Federal Aviation Administration [FAA] likely won't decide until 2015 the regulations to integrate burrito-bearing drones into urban airspace.

But the potential of a booming domestic drone industry for commercial purposes has entrepreneurs seeing dollar signs. A far stretch from the military strikes that most people typically associate with drones, developers have begun hatching a litany of ideas for unmanned air systems in the commercial sphere, controlled by civilians in American skies.

From conservation efforts and crop monitoring to Hollywood filming and even food delivery, experts anticipate the value of the commercial drone industry, already worth almost $14 billion per year, to skyrocket to more than $82 billion by

Rachel Janik and Mitchell Armentrout, "From the Burrito Bomber to Crop Monitoring, a Look at Commercial Drone Use," Medill School of Journalism Drone Project, March 19, 2013. NationalSecurityZone.Medill.Northwestern.edu. Copyright © 2013 Medill National Security Journalism Initiative. All rights reserved. Reproduced with permission.

2025, according to Mario Mairena, government relations manager for the Association for Unmanned Vehicle Systems International [AUVSI].

"And that's a conservative estimate," Mairena said. "We're excited about where the industry is at right now."

Maybe the most exciting thing is that we don't yet know all the ways this technology is going to mature.

Though opponents decry the Big Brother-like intrusion of thousands of remote cameras roaming the sky, Mairena said the industry could create as many as 70,000 jobs in the first three years after the Federal Aviation Administration releases guidelines to integrate unmanned systems into national airspace, scheduled for 2015. A recent AUVSI industry report claims that for every year commercial drone integration into the national airspace is delayed, more than $10 billion in economic potential is lost.

Chris Anderson, co-founder of drone manufacturer 3D Robotics, said he expects the commercial drone market to boom once they get clearance to enter the skies.

"Maybe the most exciting thing is that we don't yet know all the ways this technology is going to mature," he said.

Reshaping the Way We Think

One of the most promising areas for growth in unmanned systems could be in agriculture, according to Anderson.

"It's really reshaping the way we think about farming, among other things," Anderson said. Using camera-equipped drones to monitor crops could save millions per year, he said, with $300 UAVs to check for disease and irrigation levels replacing $1,000 per hour manned aircraft flyovers.

"It makes American farmers that much more competitive," he said. Hollywood is also in on the push for commercial drone licensing. Howard Gantman, spokesman for the Motion

Picture Association of America, said the film industry has been lobbying for years for the right to use unmanned aircraft for aerial filming.

"It's safer than putting a camera operator up in a tall tree, it's cheaper than renting a helicopter for a day," Gantman said.

Opening scenes from the most recent James Bond film "Skyfall" were shot from drones, as were some scenes from "The Smurfs 2." Because those were filmed in Europe, producers were able to opt for a roughly $200 drone rather than hire a helicopter filming crew for more than $2,000 per hour.

"Flight crews can eat up huge portions of movie budgets," Gantman said.

One of the more well-known uses of drones is by police departments. Steve Gitlin, spokesman for drone manufacturer AeroVironment, said law enforcement appreciate the more budget-friendly surveillance capability as an alternative to helicopters. They also have been used for search and rescue missions and deployed to locate survivors in natural disasters.

For poor countries, the ability to aerially monitor national parks and protected lands is now possible with the advent of these more affordable, model-airplane sized UAVs.

"These systems can take care of the jobs that put people in harm's way," Gitlin said.

New Weapon Against Poachers

A promising new frontier for drone surveillance could save countless endangered species, as non-profits like World Wildlife Fund [WWF] embrace UAVs to monitor wildlife populations and track poachers.

Early in 2012, WWF began research into how small UAVs like the GPS-enabled Raptor drone could help nations like Nepal stop the illegal wildlife trade. The low-cost technology has been critical in developing countries with gravely at-risk animals like the Asian elephant, white rhino and tiger. For poor countries, the ability to aerially monitor national parks and protected lands is now possible with the advent of these more affordable, model-airplane sized UAVs.

WWF's efforts have attracted attention, and the non-profit is now expanding its UAV wildlife protection programs with the help of a $5 million Global Impact Award grant from Google.

Carter Roberts, CEO [chief executive officer] of WWF, said he hoped the grant would allow animal rights groups to create "an umbrella of technology" around endangered species threatened by wildlife trafficking.

"We face an unprecedented poaching crisis. Killings are way up. We need solutions that are as sophisticated as the threats we face. This pushes the envelope in the fight against wildlife crime."

Journalistic Tools: "This Is It"

Matt Waite, professor of journalism at the University of Nebraska-Lincoln, said when he saw a drone for the first time at a digital mapping conference in 2001, he was instantly inspired.

"I thought about all the natural disasters I had covered as a reporter and I thought, 'This is it,'" he said.

Despite his enthusiasm for the new technology, using them for commercial newsgathering remains illegal in the U.S. Still, Waite was interested in pursuing UAV's potential in the industry, and set up a Drone Journalism Lab at the University of Nebraska to allow students to experiment with drones.

But the anxiety over potential privacy abuses surfaced when a false rumor surfaced that celebrity gossip site TMZ was applying for a drone of its own, presumably to get stealthy paparazzi shots of unsuspecting stars.

Waite said he believes this fear of misuse reflects more of the public's distrust of the media as a whole, not the practical application of the technology.

"Using drones in journalism does not have to include stalking Lindsay Lohan," he said. "Responsible journalists should be aware of the rules."

Waite contends that the hot topic of drones will be old news once the regulations surrounding their use are finally hashed out in both the legislature and the courts system. He predicts UAVs will be used for some of the most boring—but vital—parts of journalism, like traffic reports.

Privacy Questions Remain

For civil liberties groups, unchecked use of UAVs poses serious privacy concerns. But many private sector uses have mostly positive potential, said Electronic Privacy Information Center's Amie Stepanovich. Newsgathering in public spaces and such uses as food delivery all represent a social good as long as video footage is recorded legally and all "incidental collection" of video—footage picked up by a drone conducting a job separate from its recordings capability—is disposed of promptly, she said.

"There are definitely a lot of innovative ways to use these machines, but how do you limit what information is collected?" said Jay Stanley, an ACLU senior policy analyst. "It changes the way people feel within their environment."

Such questions have been left to the FAA, an organization that has never dealt with privacy issues until now. The drone industry awaits comprehensive guidelines, expected to be released in 2015. "We all just want rules for the road," said the University of Nebraska's Waite. "Once we have those, we can operate."

Commercial Drone Use Will Benefit the US Economy

Darryl Jenkins and Bijan Vasigh

Aviation and airline analyst Darryl Jenkins has consulted for numerous government agencies and was a member of the Executive Committee of the White House Conference on Aviation Safety and Security. Bijan Vasigh is professor of economics and finance at Embry-Riddle Aeronautical University in Daytona Beach, Florida, and a managing director at Aviation Consulting Group LLC. They wrote this viewpoint for the Association for Unmanned Vehicle Systems International (AUVSI), an organization whose mission is to advance the unmanned systems and robotics community through education, advocacy, and leadership.

The purpose of this research is to document the economic benefits to the United States (U.S.) once Unmanned Aircraft Systems (UAS) are integrated into in the National Airspace System (NAS).

In 2012, the federal government tasked the Federal Aviation Administration (FAA) to determine how to integrate UAS into the NAS. In this research, we estimate the economic impact of this integration. In the event that these regulations are delayed or not enacted, this study also estimates the jobs and financial opportunity lost to the economy because of this inaction.

While there are multiple uses for UAS in the NAS, this research concludes that precision agriculture and public safety are the most promising commercial and civil markets. These two markets are thought to comprise approximately 90% of the known potential markets for UAS.

We conclude the following:

1. The economic impact of the integration of UAS into the NAS will total more than $13.6 billion in the first three years of integration and will grow sustainably for the foreseeable future, cumulating to more than $82.1 billion between 2015 and 2025;

2. Integration into the NAS will create more than 34,000 manufacturing jobs and more than 70,000 new jobs in the first three years;

3. By 2025, total job creation is estimated at 103,776;

4. The manufacturing jobs created will be high paying ($40,000) and require Technical baccalaureate degrees;

5. Tax revenue to the states will total more than $635 billion in the first 11 years following integration (2015–2025); and

6. Every year that integration is delayed, the United States loses more than $10 billion in potential economic impact. This translates to a loss of $27.6 million per day that UAS are not integrated into the NAS.

[Unmanned Aircraft Systems] are already being used in a variety of applications, and many more areas will benefit by their use.

Utility of UAS

The main inhibitor of U.S. commercial and civil development of the UAS is the lack of a regulatory structure. Because of current airspace restrictions, non-defense use of UAS has been extremely limited. However, the combination of greater flexibility, lower capital and lower operating costs could allow UAS to be a transformative technology in fields as diverse as urban infrastructure management, farming, and oil and gas exploration to name a few.

Present-day UAS have longer operational duration and require less maintenance than earlier models. In addition, they can be operated remotely using more fuel efficient technologies. These aircraft can be deployed in a number of different terrains and may be less dependent on prepared runways. Some argue the use of UAS in the future will be a more responsible approach to certain airspace operations from an environmental, ecological and human risk perspective.

UAS are already being used in a variety of applications, and many more areas will benefit by their use, such as:

- Wildfire mapping;

- Agricultural monitoring;

- Disaster management;

- Thermal infrared power line surveys;

- Law enforcement;

- Telecommunication;

- Weather monitoring;

- Aerial imaging/mapping;

- Television news coverage, sporting events, moviemaking;

- Environmental monitoring;

- Oil and gas exploration; and

- Freight transport.

Applicable Markets

There are a number of different markets in which UAS can be used. This research is concentrated on the two markets, commercial and civil, with the largest potential. A third category (Other) summarizes all other markets:

1. Precision agriculture;

2. Public safety; and

3. Other.

Public safety officials include police officers and professional firefighters in the U.S., as well as a variety of professional and volunteer emergency medical service providers who protect the public from events that pose significant danger, including natural disasters, man-made disasters and crimes.

With sensible regulations in place, we foresee few limitations to rapid growth in [those] industries [interested in UAS].

Precision agriculture refers to two segments of the farm market: remote sensing and precision application. A variety of remote sensors are being used to scan plants for health problems, record growth rates and hydration, and locate disease outbreaks. Such sensors can be attached to ground vehicles, aerial vehicles and even aerospace satellites. Precision application, a practice especially useful for crop farmers and horticulturists, utilizes effective and efficient spray techniques to more selectively cover plants and fields. This allows farmers to provide only the needed pesticide or nutrient to each plant, reducing the total amount sprayed, and thus saving money and reducing environmental impacts.

As listed above, a large number of other markets will also use UAS once the airspace is integrated. We believe the impact of these other markets will be at least the size of the impact from public safety use.

With sensible regulations in place, we foresee few limitations to rapid growth in these industries. These products use off-the-shelf technology and thus impose few problems to rapidly ramping up production. The inputs (i.e., parts) to the UAS can be purchased from more than 100 different suppliers; therefore, prices will be stable and competitive. The inputs to the UAS can all be purchased within the U.S., although these products can be imported from any number of foreign countries without the need of an import license. UAS have a durable life span of approximately 11 years and are relatively easy to maintain. The manufacture of these products requires technical skills equivalent to a baccalaureate degree. Therefore, there will always be a plentiful market of job applicants willing to enter this market. In summary, there are no production problems on the horizon that will impact the manufacturing and output of this product. Most of the barriers of potential usage are governmental and regulatory. For this study, we assume necessary airspace integration in 2015, on par with current legislation.

States with an already thriving aerospace industry are projected to reap the most economic gains [from UAS manufacturing and use.]

Covering and justifying the cost of UAS is straightforward. In the precision agriculture market, the average price of the UAS is a fraction of the cost of a manned aircraft, such as a helicopter or crop duster, without any of the safety hazards. For public safety, the price of the product is approximately the price of a police squad car equipped with standard gear. It is also operated at a fraction of the cost of a manned aircraft, such as a helicopter, reducing the strain on agency budgets as well as the risk of bodily harm to the users in many difficult and dangerous situations. Therefore, the cost-benefit ratios of using UAS can be easily understood.

Economic Benefit

The economic benefits to the country are enormous and were estimated as follows. First, we forecast the number of sales in the three market categories. Next, we forecast the supplies needed to manufacture these products. Using estimated costs for labor, we forecast the number of direct jobs created. Using these factors, we forecast the tax revenue to the states.

In addition to direct jobs created by the manufacturing process, there is an additional economic benefit. The new jobs created and the income generated will be spread to local communities. As new jobs are created, additional money is spent at the local level, creating additional demand for local services which, in turn, creates even more jobs (i.e., grocery clerks, barbers, school teachers, home builders, etc.). These indirect and induced jobs are forecast and included in the total jobs created.

The economic benefits to individual states will not be evenly distributed. The following 10 states are predicted to see the most gains in terms of job creation and additional revenue as production of UAS increase, totaling more than $82 billion in economic impact from 2015–2025.

In rank order they are:

1. California

2. Washington

3. Texas

4. Florida

5. Arizona

6. Connecticut

7. Kansas

8. Virginia

9. New York

10. Pennsylvania

It is important to note that the projections contained in this report are based on the current airspace activity and infrastructure in a given state. As a result, states with an already thriving aerospace industry are projected to reap the most economic gains. However, a variety of factors—state laws, tax incentives, regulations, the establishment of test sites and the adoption of UAS technology by end users—will ultimately determine where jobs flow.

Job Creation

By 2025, we estimate more than 100,000 new jobs will be created nationally. For the purposes of this report, we base the 2025 state economic projections on the current aerospace employment in the states. We also presume that none of the states have enacted restrictive legislation or regulations that would limit the expansion of the technology. These landscapes will likely shift, however, as states work to attract UAS jobs in the years following integration. Future state laws and regulations could also cause some states to lose jobs while others stand to gain jobs. In conclusion, while we project more than 100,000 new jobs by 2025, states that create favorable regulatory and business environments for the industry and the technology will likely siphon jobs away from states that do not.

The trend in total spending, total economic impact and total employment impact was investigated for 2015 through 2025. The total spending in UAS development and total economic and employment impacts are expected to increase significantly in the next five years. This study demonstrates the significant contribution of UAS development and integration in the nation's airspace to the economic growth and job creation in the aerospace industry and to the social and economic progress of the citizens in the U.S.

Commercial Drone Rules Should Be Less Restrictive

Troy A. Rule

Troy A. Rule is a law professor at Arizona State University's Sandra Day O'Connor College of Law.

For more than half a century, the Federal Aviation Administration [FAA] has piloted the development of sensible aviation regulation in the United States. Unfortunately, when Congress enacted legislation in 2012 directing the FAA to craft rules for small civilian drones, the agency entered uncharted territory.

Civilian drones are fundamentally different from manned aircraft. Many small drones can be purchased online for just a few hundred dollars and are designed to hover relatively close to the ground, well below where conventional planes and helicopters fly.

The FAA is working on federal civilian drone regulations, but in the meantime, the agency has outlawed any commercial uses of drones without express FAA authorization. This ban applies to hundreds of types of flying devices that are not even capable of reaching the minimal safe altitude of manned airplanes. Several times this year, FAA officials have issued cease-and-desist notices against ordinary citizens for flying small commercial drones just a few dozen feet above land.

The FAA's controversial crackdown on commercial drones drew attention last March [2014] when an administrative law judge for the National Transportation Safety Board ruled that the FAA lacked authority to fine a man $10,000 for using his drone to capture aerial footage of the University of Virginia for a promotional video. The judge hearing the case candidly pointed out that, under the FAA's expansive view of its own regulatory power, even the flight of a paper airplane or a toy balsa wood glider would fall within FAA jurisdiction. Shockingly, an NTSB opinion issued this week reversed that decision and implied that the FAA did possess regulatory authority over the flights of unmanned objects, regardless of their size, all the way down [to] the ground.

The FAA should be focused on those aspects of drone regulation that are most appropriately implemented at the federal government level.

A Troubling Decision

This new ruling is particularly troubling because the FAA still hasn't found a federal regulatory scheme capable of effectively integrating drones into the nation's airspace. A June audit report revealed that the agency was "significantly behind schedule" in meeting congressionally imposed deadlines for its development of civilian drone regulations. Frustrated at the FAA's snail-like pace, companies such as Amazon and Google have begun exporting their drone research activities to other countries.

Small drones are not built for lengthy interstate flights at altitudes where conventional airplanes fly, so why should a federal agency be the chief regulator of these devices? Rather than seeking to expand its regulatory jurisdiction all the way down to the ground, the FAA should advocate for itself a more limited role in a collaborative federal, state and local regulatory scheme tailored to the unique attributes of drone technologies.

A "Geo-Fence" for Safety

The FAA should be focused on those aspects of drone regulation that are most appropriately implemented at the federal government level. For instance, the agency could accelerate the development of national drone safety and performance standards analogous to the National Highway Traffic Safety Administration's manufacturing standards for motor vehicles. Among other things, these FAA standards could require that all commercial drones incorporate specific global positioning system features to ensure compatibility with a nationally standardized geo-fence network designed to keep drones out of the way of conventional aircraft. At least one leading drone manufacturer is already using "geo-fence" software to prevent operators from flying their drones into the airspace surrounding hundreds of airports around the world.

Most other facets of civilian drone regulation are better suited for lower levels of government. Several state legislatures have already enacted drone-related statutes, but states should be doing much more. In addition to creating registration and licensing programs for commercial drones and their operators, legislatures could enact laws that clarify the scope of landowners' rights to exclude drones from the airspace directly above their land. If tailored properly, these aerial trespass statutes could help to address a wide array of conflicts involving drones, including those involving law enforcement uses of drone devices.

Drone Zone Laws

Local governments are well-positioned to serve valuable functions in drone regulation as well. In particular, drone zoning laws adopted at the local level could permit wider use of drones in certain commercial or agricultural zones while imposing greater restrictions on drones above residential areas. Municipalities could even adopt temporary-use permit provisions to accommodate occasional drone use by real estate agents and wedding photographers without compromising landowner privacy. Regrettably, until the FAA signals that it does not intend to regulate these sorts of activities at the federal level, most local officials are unlikely to craft innovative drone policies within their communities.

The commercial drone industry is poised to take off in the United States, but it will largely remain grounded until the FAA embraces a narrower regulatory role and gets out of the way.

Banning Commercial Drones Is Not the Answer

Vivek Wadhwa

Vivek Wadhwa is a fellow at the Rock Center for Corporate Governance at Stanford University and director of research at the Center for Entrepreneurship and Research Commercialization at Duke University.

The Federal Aviation Administration recently released a report detailing more than 190 safety incidents involving drones and commercial aircraft. In response, Senator Dianne Feinstein (D-Calif.) has vowed to push legislation that would crack down on the commercial use of drones, also called Unmanned Aircraft Systems (UAS). India's Directorate General for Civil Aviation has already banned all use of drones in the country—even for civilian purposes.

There are valid concerns that the proliferation of drones will endanger commercial flights and cause serious accidents. The U.S. military is rightfully worried that drones will be weaponized as killing machines and become autonomous flying IEDs (improvised explosive devices) that target a specific individual by means of facial recognition.

Banning commercial drone use will not solve these problems; it will just give us a false sense of comfort and kick the can further down the road.

About two years ago, I wrote a *Washington Post* column in which I argued that we need to prepare ourselves for the "drone age." It isn't just the United States that is developing drone capabilities; governments and DIYers all over the world are doing the same, particularly the Chinese. This isn't all bad; there are many good uses for drone technologies.

To start with, there isn't yet a clear consensus on what a drone is. Is it something that flies and is remote controlled? If that is the case, should the FAA also ban remote-controlled airplanes and helicopters that hobbyists have flown happily and relatively safely for many years? The drone encounter that Senator Feinstein cited in a Senate Commerce Committee hearing as a reason to regulate commercial drone flights was reportedly just a pink toy helicopter.

Let's first acknowledge that drones will be common in our skies and that they will play an integral role in our economy and society.

Would Drone Bans Be Enforceable?

Then there is the practicability of enforcement. If the government should institute restrictions and penalties, who will enforce them? Will the police buy high-performance drones to shoot down illicit drones? Can we scramble the Air Force to blow a flock of $300 quadcopters out of the sky? Should we equip legions of young children with air rifles? Proposing laws without realistic hope of enforcement does nothing to solve the problems at hand.

Let's first acknowledge that drones will be common in our skies and that they will play an integral role in our economy and society. We know that drones are saving money and improving safety on many types of remote inspection such as that of distant pipelines and tall broadcast towers. Documentary filmmakers use drones to get aerial shots that are not affordable with a regular plane or helicopter. As well, start-ups like Matternet are pioneering the use of drones to deliver critical medical supplies to remote parts of the developing world. Drones could be used as long-haul cargo-delivery vehicles, allowing for more efficient point-to-point delivery of goods and materials. Then of course, companies such as Google and Amazon are developing drone delivery services that provide within-the-hour delivery of ordered goods— without putting any more traffic onto the streets or carbon into the skies.

So if we don't ban the drones, what can we do to prepare for them and weave their capabilities into a broader picture of economic development?

Collision-Avoidance Technology Is a Challenge

First, there needs to be a core technology framework for collision avoidance. This is no small problem. Even the best computer-vision algorithms struggle to navigate complex cityscapes. The vehicles in NASA's DARPA challenge weighed thousands of pounds and carried serious computational and sensor firepower. Yet they could barely navigate barren wastelands without flipping themselves over or running into a wall. So how will a drone the size of a shoebox carry enough intelligence to avoid hitting a building, a person, a car, a power line or, worst case, a commercial aircraft? It's a wonderful engineering challenge and worth the focus of some of our best minds.

Assuming we have collision-avoidance systems in place, how can we build a system of distributed air-traffic control for drones? It would obviously need to be computer-driven and automatic, and to include safety measures and emergency kill switches or other mechanisms to bring down a drone that is malfunctioning or poses a danger. We would need to plan for specific air corridors in city areas that are dedicated to drones and confine the drones to those places. Again, this is a huge engineering challenge, but not one that is insurmountable.

More Problems to Solve

We also need to build private and commercial air-defense systems, just as the military is developing, to shield our schools, homes, and businesses from drone surveillance or attack. I wonder whether force fields such as we saw on *Star Trek* may become a practical reality.

Beyond the technical issues, we need to debate what is socially acceptable and to create legal frameworks. Should the cameras of delivery drones be recording and saving all video footage as they enter into the airspace of a customer's home? For that matter, should drones be allowed to fly over private property at all—or should they be limited to public roads between droneports? Should we have the right to shoot down unauthorized drones on our property? If the Second Amendment grants the right of gun ownership to individuals for self-defense, then does it allow them to fly their own defensive drones?

These are issues we need to tackle—and soon. The drones are coming, whether we are ready or not.

Commercial Drones Could Threaten National Security

Michael McCaul

Texas Republican Michael McCaul is chairman of the US House of Representatives Subcommittee on Oversight, Investigations, and Management.

Unmanned aerial systems [UAS], commonly known as "drones," have been a game changer for our men and women serving in Iraq and Afghanistan. These systems have provided our troops with much needed "eyes in the sky" and have taken the fight to the enemy, eliminating some of the most dangerous Al-Qaeda terrorists. Drones have also increased our capabilities to secure our borders and aid first responders.

US Customs and Border Protection [CBP] began first looking at using drones back in 2004. Now, CBP owns ten UAS aircraft. These systems have been used to surveil drug smuggling tunnels; video dams, bridges, levees, and riverbeds at risk of flooding; and assist with the deployment of National Guard resources responding to local flooding. CBP has flown missions in support of the Border Patrol, Texas Rangers, US Forest Service, FBI [Federal Bureau of Investigation], and others. These systems have become a force multiplier for military operations and border security.

However, we are now on the edge of a new horizon: using unmanned aerial systems within the homeland. Currently, there are about 200 active Certificates of Authorization issued by the Federal Aviation Administration [FAA] to over 100 dif-

Michael McCaul, "Using Unmanned Aerial Systems Within the Homeland: Security Game Changer?," Statement to the House Subcommittee on Oversight, Investigations, and Management, July 19, 2012.

ferent entities, such as law enforcement departments and academic institutions, to fly drones domestically. . . .

The FAA plans to select six test sites around the country for the use of non-government drones this year and plans to allow the deployment of non-government drones nationwide by 2015.

The US government [is] concerned that these aerial vehicles could be modified and used to attack key assets and critical infrastructure in the United States.

Government Agencies Are Lagging

While the FAA is responsible for ensuring these systems fly safely in US airspace, with only two and a half short years until drones begin to dominate the skies in the US homeland, no federal agency is taking the lead to deal with the full implications of using unmanned aerial systems and developing the relevant policies and guidelines for their use. This is despite the fact that four years ago the Government Accountability Office [GAO] recommended the Secretary of Homeland Security direct the TSA Administrator to examine the security implications of future, non-military UAS operations in the national airspace system and take any actions deemed appropriate.

GAO's recommendation was well founded because in 2004 TSA issued an advisory that described possible terrorist interest in using UASs as weapons. The advisory noted the potential for UASs to carry explosives or disperse chemical or biological weapons. It discussed how the Revolutionary Armed Forces of Columbia, or FARC, and Hezbollah were interested in acquiring UASs. While the advisory acknowledged there was no credible evidence to suggest that terrorist organizations planned to use these systems in the United States, it did state that the US government was concerned that these aerial vehicles could be modified and used to attack key assets and critical infrastructure in the United States.

Drones Pose Potential Threats

These concerns were validated just last week [July 2012] when a Massachusetts man agreed to plead guilty to attempting to damage and destroy federal buildings. The individual was arrested in September 2011 after an undercover FBI investigation revealed his plot to use multiple remote controlled aircraft laden with explosives to collapse the dome of the US Capitol and attack the Pentagon.

As if this plot wasn't frightening enough, cutting edge research out of the University of Texas at Austin has revealed yet more security vulnerabilities. Specifically, researchers from the Cockrell School of Engineering led by Dr. Todd Humphreys proved that civilian unmanned aerial systems can be hacked into and hijacked with a relatively small investment of money and time. These findings are alarming and have revealed a gaping hole in the security of using unmanned aerial systems domestically. Now is the time to ensure these vulnerabilities are mitigated to protect our aviation system as the use of unmanned aerial systems continues to grow.

The Department of Homeland Security [DHS] mission is to protect the homeland. Unfortunately, DHS seems either disinterested or unprepared to step up to the plate to address the proliferation of Unmanned Aerial Systems in US air space, the potential threats they pose to our national security, and the concerns of our citizens of how drones flying over our cities will be used including protecting civil liberties of individuals under the Constitution. For example, in discussions with my Subcommittee staff prior to this hearing, Department officials repeatedly stated the Department does not see this function (domestic use of drones) as part of their mission and has no role in domestic unmanned aerial systems. I strongly disagree.

A Call to Action

DHS's lack of attention about this issue is incomprehensible. It should not take a 9/11 style attack by a terrorist organization such as Hezbollah or a lone wolf inspired event to cause DHS to develop guidance addressing the security implications of domestic drones. It should not take a hearing to force DHS to develop policy when it comes to the security of our homeland. What it should take is responsible leadership willing to recognize a potential threat and take the initiative. DHS lacks that initiative. I am concerned DHS is reverting back to a pre-9/11 mindset, which the 9/11 Commission described as a lack of imagination in identifying threats and protecting the homeland.

We are disappointed DHS declined to testify today. This is simply another example of how DHS leadership is failing to get ahead of the curve on an issue which directly impacts the security of the United States. I hope that our witnesses' testimony will be a call to action for the Department. During today's testimony, we look forward to learning more about the security issues related to the domestic use of drones and what DHS needs to do to prepare for their widespread use.

Weaponized Hobby Drones Are Inevitable

Patrick Hruby

Award-winning journalist Patrick Hruby is an adjunct professor at Georgetown University and a fellow at the University of Texas.

Less than a month ago [December 2012], rumors that celebrity news and gossip website TMZ was interested in obtaining a paparazzi drone prompted privacy concerns and public debate about the appropriate personal and commercial uses of unmanned aerial vehicles.

Now, a new online video poses a more troubling question: What if civilian drones are equipped to shoot more than just pictures?

Titled "Citizen Drone Warfare" and posted to YouTube last week by an anonymous man calling himself "Milo Danger," the video shows a hobbyist drone equipped with a custom-mounted paintball pistol flying over a grassy field and peppering human-shaped shooting-range targets with pellets.

Following an attack pass by the drone, one of the targets sports three large red blotches on its head and neck area.

"I wanted to show an inevitability of what I think will happen with these drones," said "Milo," who lives on the West Coast and spoke to *The Washington Times* on condition of anonymity. "I'm not advocating bad activities. But I wanted to raise some of the ethical issues we need to think about with this new technology.

"We didn't post the footage of this, but some of the guys who worked with me on the project weren't afraid of being shot by paintballs. They wanted to see if they could escape the drone. The answer was, no, they could not."

Though Federal Aviation Administration [FAA] regulations do not explicitly mention the use of firearms on drones, they do prohibit any type of recreational flying or dropping objects from aircraft that endanger life or property.

The Drone Community Reacts

DIYDrones.com, a drone hobbyist website and online community that counts defense and aerospace engineers among its 32,000 members and averages more than 1.5 million page views a month, discourages using or modifying drones for any uses that are "potentially illegal or intended to do harm."

Defense experts have warned for years that small, commercially available drones could be used as weapons.

"We've banned the weaponized use of drones," said Chris Anderson, the site's founder. "So in our community, the reaction to this video is dismay. We're particularly interested in civilian uses of drones, things like search-and-rescue and filming sports teams. Obviously, putting a paintball gun on a drone doesn't help."

American Civil Liberties Union [ACLU] policy analyst Jay Stanley wrote on the organization's website that the video was "pretty scary" and America "cannot allow our skies to fill with flying robots armed with all manner of dangerous weapons."

Mr. Stanley also noted that defense experts have warned for years that small, commercially available drones could be used as weapons. In 2004, a New Zealand engineer managed to build a miniature cruise missile for less than $5,000, a project that subsequently was shut down by the nation's government because of security concerns.

Last month, a 27-year-old Massachusetts man was sentenced to 17 years in prison for plotting to attack the Pentagon and the Capitol with a remote-controlled model aircraft rigged with explosives.

"We've called for a ban on armed drones, and I think there's a broad consensus that we should not allow armed drones to be used domestically," said Mr. Stanley, the author of a report on drones and privacy. "The International Association of Chiefs of Police has recommended against it. I think this video likely will further cement that consensus."

"Terrifyingly Easy"

In the video, Milo wears sunglasses, a black baseball cap, a large American-flag bandanna that covers his face and a T-shirt reading "Dangerous Information"—the latter the name of a fledgling Web video series that explores topics such as picking locks and growing marijuana.

Holding a small, six-rotor hobbyist drone in his hand, Milo states that the realistic-looking handgun attached to the machine's undercarriage fires "non-lethal" 11 mm paintballs.

By the time the drone lands, [it] has hit all five targets repeatedly.

"Let me be clear, under no circumstances should you ever put a live firearm on a drone, a remote-controlled toy or any other vehicle," he says. "It's incredibly dangerous.

"Can a mail-order drone from a kit even handle the stress of rounds cycling through a gun? Is it accurate? Let's find out."

Flying about 15 feet above the ground and controlled by Milo with the help of an onboard video camera that transmits real-time images to a set of piloting goggles, the drone maneuvers around five human-shaped targets, the buzz of its electric engines mixing with the popping sound of the paintball gun discharging.

By the time the drone lands, Milo has hit all five targets repeatedly.

"If the question is, 'How easy is it to fly this drone?' the answer is, 'terrifyingly easy,'" he said. "The first time we flew it, we were able to put all of the paintball ammunition into a target 50 yards away from the operator—and 15 yards from the [drone]—in an area the size of a dinner plate."

Do-It-Yourself Drone Training

According to Milo, building the drone was nearly as straightforward. He purchased the drone and the paintball gun online, downloaded open-source piloting software and found instructions on how to get the drone up and running by running simple Internet searches for the terms "drones" and "DIY."

The entire project, he said, took no more than a dozen hours and cost less than $2,000.

"I'm not particularly handy," he said. "But I was able pick up this pretty high-end hobby as a completely inexperienced person and master it with a small budget in a couple of weeks. It was up and flying within a couple of sessions of working on it, and that's including trial and error and making mistakes."

The hardest part, Milo said, was centering the weight of the paintball pistol, which weighs approximately 2 pounds—roughly the same weight as many actual handguns.

"There would be some practical physical considerations to mounting a real gun," Milo said. "Many pistols have significantly greater recoil. However, some guns have very little. And the onboard computer for the drone tries to keep itself level even if you try to knock it out of the air.

"I don't think it would have problems staying in the air with many smaller firearms, but I don't encourage anyone doing that."

Unlike the autonomous human-hunting drones of dystopian science fiction—think "The Terminator" film series—Milo's drone flew by remote control [RC], the same way miniature dune buggies and toy airplanes are piloted by RC enthusiasts.

"With very little extra work, however, we could program it on a computer to fly on a path, fire on a fixed target and then fly home with little human intervention," he said. "This drone is capable of that."

The Future Is Soon?

Earlier this year, a different YouTube video appeared to show a homemade quad-rotor drone with a custom-mounted machine gun laying explosive waste to a group of mannequins.

The fun and valid uses of this technology are going to happen. But other possibilities are there.

Viewed more than 15 million times, the video turned out to be a hoax, part of a viral marketing campaign for the future-warfare video game "Call of Duty: Black Ops II."

"Drones are a hot topic," Milo said. "You can't look at the Internet without coming across a drone-related story. Most of them are about military drones or government and police agencies considering drones and their uses. But very infrequently do you see stories that cover the DIY maker approach.

"The fun and valid uses of this technology are going to happen. But other possibilities are there. Surveillance drones over American skies. Armed drones. Not just your local police but also your neighbors. I wanted to create a video that put the questions out there."

For the most part, drones currently are confined to the military—which reportedly has more than 7,500 vehicles in service—and hobbyists such as Milo, who are flying roughly double that number. Moreover, current FAA rules largely prohibit commercial drone use, while hobbyists are subject to strict guidelines: no flying above 400 feet, near populated areas or outside the operator's line of sight.

A federal law passed in February [2012], however, compels the FAA to allow drone use by police and emergency services later this year and allow "safe" commercial use by September 2015.

Video Sparks Consumer Interest

Drone advocates such as Mr. Anderson argue that the technology is akin to the personal computer, flexible enough to perform important and useful tasks ranging from crop-dusting to inspecting pipelines to extreme sports photography.

Milo said excited paintball players began contacting him within hours of his video being posted online.

"A ton of people are very excited, to the point of 'Shut up and take my money' and 'This is now on my Christmas list,'" he said. "People are interested in playing with this kind of toy."

Acknowledging the inevitability of increased drone use by the government and private citizens alike, Mr. Stanley said society needs to proceed with caution.

The Washington Times recently reported that because of privacy issues, the FAA appears likely to miss its self-imposed Dec. 31 deadline to choose six sites in states throughout the nation where drones will be put through a battery of safety and other tests before full commercialization is allowed.

"There is nothing like seeing actual video of something that might be an abstract concept to bring home the reality of the fast-paced technological era we are living in," Mr. Stanley said. "And this video is a reminder of how we really need to step up and deal with these issues, and not just sit back and let things happen on their own. Whether that's preventing guns from being placed on drones, or putting in rules to protect our privacy, we should decide if these are changes we want or don't want and protect ourselves as necessary."

Commercial Drones Must Be Thoroughly Regulated

Arthur Holland Michel

Arthur Holland Michel is codirector of the Center for the Study of the Drone at Bard College in New York, an interdisciplinary research, education, and art community working to understand unmanned and autonomous vehicles.

In 2012, when small drones, the kind that weigh just a few pounds and carry a small object (like a camera, or a burrito) became affordable, the idea of a drone-filled airspace began shifting from sci-fi fantasy to reality. But the passage toward integration was set to be turbulent.

Drones were more commonly thought of as the weaponized, ghostlike military spy aircraft that lurked over Pakistan, Yemen and Somalia, killing enemy militants and, occasionally, civilians and children. While these drones have little in common with small domestic drones, the public was spooked. Groups like the American Civil Liberties Union [ACLU] raised alarms. Fearing for privacy and safety, lawmakers from Washington state to Virginia rushed to propose legislation to limit or ban drones, even very small ones. The Federal Aviation Administration [FAA] stressed, sternly, that commercial drone use would be absolutely prohibited until 2015, when it would enact comprehensive—and strict—safety regulations. The agency reminded the public that private drone users were subject to restrictions, too.

Two years later, the drones are soaring, while the efforts to limit their use have stalled and the public debate has gone into a tailspin.

Arthur Holland Michel, "The Drones Will Have Their Day," *U.S. News & World Report*, August 6, 2014. USNews.com. Copyright © 2014 U.S. News & World Report. All rights reserved. Reproduced with permission.

In June [2014], a company called Squadrone System started a Kickstarter campaign to fund a small multi-rotor drone called the HEXO+, which the company described as "an intelligent drone that follows and films you autonomously," perfect for making exciting action sports videos. Within a few hours, the campaign had raised more than three times its $50,000 target. When the campaign ended, the company had raised $1.3 million.

In state legislatures, drone regulation is one of the few issues that has enjoyed bipartisan support.

Drone Fever vs. Drone Fear

That same week, a company called APlus Mobile made its own Kickstarter campaign. Instead of a drone, the company proposed a Personal Drone Detection System—essentially, an anti-drone radar. "Our intent is to keep your privacy safe from your neighbors and people you may not know who are flying small drones near your home or office," it said. The campaign only managed to raise $1,435 of its $8,500 goal. It's clear: The drone is winning.

In state legislatures, drone regulation is one of the few issues that has enjoyed bipartisan support. In 2013, according to the ACLU, 43 states debated 96 drone bills; however, all but eight of these bills died in session. This year, just four out of 36 states that considered drone legislation have enacted any laws. This is not enough to keep pace with drone proliferation.

And lawmakers in Washington aren't jumping to regulate the drone. In fact, some have caught drone fever. Last month [July 2014], Democratic Rep. Sean Patrick Maloney of New York hired a photographer who used a drone to capture (admittedly rather stunning) aerial views of the congressman's wedding. Sen. Rand Paul, R-Ky., who filibustered Congress for

13 hours in protest of government drone use, owns a toy drone. When he flew it on Fox News, the look on his face was childlike.

Recommendations, Not Regulations

Even the FAA has been toothless. Desperate to prevent the midair meeting of a drone and a manned aircraft, the agency has released a number of policy statements intended to limit unsafe drone use. These statements include the ban on commercial use. But policy statements are not legally binding. They are recommendations, placeholders for the real, legally enforceable regulations that will come sometime after 2015. While private individuals and companies often respect federal agency policy statements, in the case of the FAA, droners, eager to get airborne, have openly flaunted them.

The FAA has attempted to enforce these policy statements through cease-and-desist letters and, in one case, a $10,000 fine. But these actions have been repeatedly struck down in court. The FAA's attempts at enforcement have therefore only served to highlight that it has its hands tied. Meanwhile, the rules that actually are legal (like keeping away from airports) are easy to break and difficult to enforce.

> *The domestic integration of drones must not be rushed. . . . The FAA needs time to develop an integration plan, a gargantuan task that will (and should) take several years.*

At an industry level, the FAA and the droners have fallen into the all-too-familiar battle that pits regulation against the profit-efficiency motive. The drone industry, represented formally by the Association for Unmanned Vehicle Systems International, is frustrated that the FAA's foot-dragging is keeping the U.S. from launching into what will be a multibillion dollar industry. When I visited the association's annual trade show in May, people talked about the FAA as if it was a regulatory boogeyman.

The coexistence of federal regulations and a profit-hungry industry is never a happy one. "Each day that integration is delayed will lead to $27 million in lost economic impact," wrote Michael Toscano, the association's president, in a letter to the FAA in January. Mathematical fuzziness aside, the argument misses a point: Well-thought-out safety regulations, especially in the air, where stakes are high, have no price. Two years ago, this battle would have been unthinkable.

Addressing Complex Challenges Will Take Time

When used intelligently, or by professionals, drones are safe and useful. Recently, an amateur drone pilot found his lost grandfather in just 20 minutes; the authorities had been searching for three days. But if used stupidly, drones are dangerous. Just a few days after the missing grandfather was retrieved, Cal Fire almost had to suspend operations over the Plymouth wildfires because an amateur videographer was flying a drone in the area. Just because pretty much anybody can fly a drone doesn't mean that everybody should. The dangers of improper drone use are real.

The domestic integration of drones must not be rushed. It is naturally a challenging process, because drones present a set of complex challenges. The FAA needs time to develop an integration plan, a gargantuan task that will (and should) take several years. Safety ought to have priority over profits.

Calls for caution are not alarmism; they are legitimate. A vigorous and balanced debate in state assemblies, on Capitol Hill and in public forums is prerequisite to the development of sensible policies and norms. We are not seeing that debate. It has been squelched by the technological promise of kits like the HEXO+.

Alluring as it is, let's not get carried away with the drone. As the technology develops more quickly and the price drops further, the safety and privacy concerns will become more pressing. We need to be careful and patient. The drone will have its day. Let's make sure we are prepared for it when it does.

Organizations to Contact

The editors have compiled the following list of organizations concerned with the issues debated in this book. The descriptions are derived from materials provided by the organizations. All have publications or information available for interested readers. The list was compiled on the date of publication of the present volume; the information provided here may change. Be aware that many organizations take several weeks or longer to respond to inquiries, so allow as much time as possible.

American Civil Liberties Union (ACLU)
125 Broad St., 18th Floor, New York, NY   10004
(212) 549-2500
e-mail: info@aclu.org
website: www.aclu.org

Through activism in courts, legislatures, and communities nationwide, the American Civil Liberties Union (ACLU) works to defend the individual rights and liberties that the Constitution and laws of the United States guarantee to everyone. The ACLU website has an extensive collection of reports, briefings, and news updates related to the use of drones, with an emphasis on concerns about human rights, privacy, mass surveillance, police militarization, and civil liberties. Publications available from the ACLU include "Unchecked Government Drones? Not Over My Backyard," "The Unreal Secrecy About Drone Killings," and "ACLU Testifies on the Need for Regulation of Surveillance by Domestic Drones."

American Security Project (ASP)
1100 New York Ave. NW, Suite 710W, Washington, DC   20005
(202) 347-4267
website: http://americansecurityproject.org

The American Security Project (ASP) believes that America's current national security strategy is flawed and that it increases worldwide anti-Americanism and threatens the nation's ability to compete in the global marketplace. The organization hopes to increase public awareness of the true nature of the struggle between the United States and violent extremists so that the country might develop more effective policies and strategies to meet the threat. On its website, ASP publishes issue summaries, recent issues of *American Security Quarterly*, and reports, including *Understanding the Strategies and Tactical Considerations of Drone Strikes*. Under the link Issues/ Asymmetric Operations/Strategic Effect of Drones, ASP publishes an annotated bibliography on drones.

Amnesty International USA

5 Penn Plaza, New York, NY 10001
(212) 807-8400 • fax: (212) 627-1451
e-mail: aimember@aiusa.org
website: www.amnestyusa.org

Amnesty International USA works to ensure that governments do not deny individuals their basic human rights as outlined in the United Nations Universal Declaration of Human Rights. The organization seeks greater transparency in the use of drones and opposes targeted killing without due process. Its website contains recent news, reports, and a searchable database of archived publications, including many on the impact of drones and drone policies.

Association for Unmanned Vehicle Systems International (AUVSI)

2700 S. Quincy St., Suite 400, Arlington, VA 22206
(703) 845-9671 • fax: (703) 845-9679
e-mail: info@auvsi.org
website: www.auvsi.org

The Association for Unmanned Vehicle Systems International (AUVSI) is a membership organization that supports the use of unmanned aerial systems such as drones and related technology. Members represent government organizations, industry, and academia and support the defense, civil, and commercial sectors. AUVSI publishes the monthly magazine *Unmanned*

Systems, which highlights current global developments and unveils new technologies in air, ground, maritime, and space systems, and *Mission Critical,* a quarterly electronic publication. The organization's website features extensive information about drones and other unmanned systems, regulatory efforts, and related issues.

Brookings Institution

1775 Massachusetts Ave. NW, Washington, DC   20036
(202) 797-6000 • fax: (202) 797-6004
e-mail: communications@brookings.edu
website: www.brookings.edu

Founded in 1927, the Brookings Institution conducts research and analyzes global events and their impact on the United States and US foreign policy. It publishes the quarterly *Brookings Review* and numerous books and research papers. Its website publishes editorials, papers, testimony, reports, and articles written by Brookings scholars, including "The Global Swarm: An International Drone Market," "The Predator Comes Home: A Primer on Domestic Drones, Their Huge Business Opportunities, and Their Deep Political, Moral, and Legal Challenges," and "When Can the US Target Alleged American Terrorists Overseas?"

Cato Institute

1000 Massachusetts Ave. NW, Washington, DC   2001-5403
(202) 842-0200 • fax: (202) 842-3490
website: www.cato.org

The Cato Institute is a libertarian public policy research foundation dedicated to peace and limited government intervention in domestic and foreign affairs. Cato publishes numerous reports and periodicals, including *Policy Analysis* and *Cato Policy Report,* both of which discuss US drone policy as both a domestic and foreign policy tool. Its website contains a searchable database of Institute articles, news, multimedia, and commentary, including the video "Game of Drones: Liberty and Security in the Age of Flying Robots" and the article "Look up in the Sky and See a Drone."

Center for Strategic and International Studies (CSIS)

CSIS Center for Strategic and International Studies
Washington, DC   20036
(202) 887-0200 • fax: (202) 775-3199
website: www.csis.org

The Center for Strategic and International Studies (CSIS) conducts research and develops policy recommendations on a variety of issues, including defense and security strategies, economic development, energy and climate change, global health, technology, and trade. The Center publishes *The Washington Quarterly*, recent articles from which are available at its website. CSIS publishes books, reports, newsletters, and commentaries targeted at decision makers in government, business, and academia. Website visitors can access articles on drones through the website's search engine, including "US Civil Drone Policy" and "The Alternatives to Drone Strikes Are Worse."

Council on Foreign Relations (CFR)

58 East 68th St., New York, NY   10021
(212) 434-9400 • fax: (212) 434-9800
e-mail: communications@cfr.org
website: www.cfr.org

The Council on Foreign Relations (CFR) specializes in foreign affairs and studies the international aspects of American political and economic policies and problems. Its journal *Foreign Affairs*, published five times a year, includes analyses of current conflicts around the world. Its website publishes editorials, interviews, articles, and reports, including the article "Why Did the CIA Stop Torturing and Start Killing?" and the report "Reforming US Drone Strike Policies."

Drone Project/Medill National Security Journalism Initiative

Medill School of Journalism
Media Integrated Marketing Communications
Evanston, IL   60208-2101
(847) 467-1882

e-mail: contact@nationalsecurityzone.org
website: http://droneproject.nationalsecurityzone.org

The Drone Project is part of the Medill National Security Journalism Initiative, a program at Northwestern University that provides working journalists and those in training with the knowledge and skills to report accurately, completely, and with context on issues related to defense, security, and civil liberties. The Drone Project website features dozens of informative articles about drones and drone policy written by student reporters, many of which have been published by McClatchy newspapers. The Drone Project website also features an interactive map that details the current status of drone legislation in each state.

Drone Safety Council (DSC)

e-mail: info@dronesafetycouncil.org
website: http://dronesafetycouncil.com

Formed in 2013, the Drone Safety Council (DSC) is an industry-standards body working to develop safety standards for commercial and civilian drones and unmanned robotic vehicles. The nonprofit organization is dedicated to addressing the growing concerns for the safety of commercial and civilian drone operators as well as the general public. The group's goal is to inform, investigate, and implement drone safety standards that will be adopted by drone manufacturers and by global governments for the safety of all concerned. The DSC website includes a wide variety of information about drone safety and current and pending regulations, in addition to updates on the group's efforts.

Human Rights Watch

350 Fifth Ave., 34th Floor, New York, NY 10118-3299
(212) 290-4700 • fax: (212) 736-1300
e-mail: hrwnyc@hrw.org
website: www.hrw.org

Founded in 1978, Human Rights Watch is a nongovernmental organization that conducts systematic investigations of human rights abuses in countries around the world. It publishes many books and reports on specific countries and issues as well as annual reports, recent selections of which are available at its website. Publications on drones include "What Rules Should Govern US Drone Attacks?," "A Dangerous Model: The US Should Reveal Its Legal Rationale for Drone Attacks," and "Anatomy of an Air Attack Gone Wrong."

The Rutherford Institute

PO Box 7482, Charlottesville, VA   22966-7482
(434) 978-3888
e-mail: staff@rutherford.org
website: www.rutherford.org

The Rutherford Institute is a conservative civil liberties think tank with a dual mission. It provides legal services in the defense of religious and civil liberties and seeks to educate the public on important issues affecting constitutional freedoms. The Institute supports strong civil liberties protections from constitutional invasions by domestic drones. Its website publishes news and commentary on the domestic use of drones, including "Key Cases: Drones" and "Roaches, Mosquitoes, and Birds: The Coming Micro-Drone Revolution," and commentary by its founder, constitutional attorney John W. Whitehead.

Bibliography

Books

Medea Benjamin   *Drone Warfare*. New York: OR Books, 2012.

Marjorie Cohn, ed.   *Drones and Targeted Killing: Legal, Moral, and Geopolitical Issues*. Charles City, VA: Olive Branch, 2014.

David Cortright, Rachel Fairhurst, and Kristen Wall, eds.   *Drones and the Future of Armed Conflict: Ethical, Legal, and Strategic Implications*. Chicago: University of Chicago Press, 2015.

Steven Hogan   *The Drone Revolution: How Robotic Aviation Will Change the World*. Seattle: CreateSpace, 2015.

Craig Issod   *Getting Started with Hobby Quadcopters and Drones: Learn About, Buy and Fly These Amazing Aerial Vehicles*. Seattle: CreateSpace, 2013.

Mark LaFay   *Drones for Dummies*. New York: Wiley & Sons, 2015.

Jerry LeMieux   *Drone Entrepreneurship: 30 Businesses You Can Start*. Phoenix, AZ: Unmanned Vehicle University Press, 2013.

Jonathan Rupprecht   *Drones: Their Many Civilian Uses and the US Laws Surrounding Them*. Seattle: CreateSpace, 2015.

P.W. Singer — *Wired for War: The Robotics Revolution and Conflict in the 21st Century*. New York: Penguin, 2009.

Richard Whittle — *Predator: The Secret Origins of the Drone Revolution*. New York: Henry Holt and Co., 2014.

Periodicals and Internet Sources

Hassan Abbas — "Are Drone Strikes Killing Terrorists or Creating Them?," *Atlantic*, March 31, 2013.

Hassan Abbas — "How Drones Create More Terrorists," *Atlantic*, August 23, 2013.

Amnesty International — "Will I Be Next? US Drone Strikes in Pakistan," amnestyusa.org, 2013. www.amnestyusa.org.

Associated Press — "Drone 'Containing Radiation' Lands on Roof of Japanese PM's Office in Tokyo," *Guardian* (UK), April 22, 2015.

Associated Press — "Poll: Americans Skeptical of Commercial Drones," *Toledo Blade*, December 19, 2014.

Kelsey Atherton — "FAA May Never Figure out Drone Rules," *Popular Science*, June 30, 2014.

Kelsey Atherton — "This Is the FAA's Plan for Drone-Friendly Skies," *Popular Science*, November 8, 2013.

Ashley Balcerzak and Taylor Hiegel   "Police Forces Struggle to Incorporate Drones," Medill School of Journalism Drone Project, March 18, 2013. http://droneproject.nationalsecurityzone.org.

Jeremy Barr   "Journalists Await New Drone Regulations. And Wait, and Wait . . . ," poynter.org, January 30, 2014. www.poynter.org.

Tom Barry   "Fallacies of High-Tech Fixes for Border Security—International Policy Report," Center for International Policy, April 2010. www.ciponline.org.

Tom Barry   "How the Drone Warfare Industry Took Over Our Congress," AlterNet, November 30, 2011. www.alternet.org.

Peter Bergen and Jennifer Rowland   "A Dangerous New World of Drones," CNN, October 8, 2012. www.cnn.com.

Rae Ellen Bichell   "No Seat Belts Required: Drone Hobbyists Talk Safety," National Public Radio, October 26, 2013. www.npr.org.

Matt Bigler   "Controversial Police Drone Inches Closer to Flight in San Jose," cbslocal.com, April 9, 2015. http://sanfrancisco.cbslocal.com.

Thomas Black   "Armed Drones Seen as Dogfight-Ready in (Not-Too-Distant) Future," Bloomberg Business, May 8, 2015. www.bloomberg.com.

Joshua Bleiberg   "Drones and Aerial Surveillance: The Opportunities and the Risks," Brookings Institution, November 18, 2014. www.brookings.edu.

Joshua Bleiberg   "Should Rock Bands Use Drones?," Brookings Institution, November 5, 2014. www.brookings.edu.

Bloomberg Business   "Alibaba Drones Fly Over Beijing While Amazon Pleads for US Tests," February 2, 2015. www.bloomberg.com.

Allie Bohm   "Drone Legislation: What's Being Proposed in the States?," ACLU, March 6, 2013. www.aclu.org.

Cory Booker   "Can US Drone Policy Finally Soar?," CNN, February 19, 2015. www.cnn.com.

William Booth   "More Predators Fly US Border," *Washington Post*, December 1, 2011.

Rod Boshart   "Carter: US Drone Attacks Violate Human Rights," *Quad-City Times*, September 14, 2012.

Christopher Calabrese   "The Future of Unmanned Aviation in the U.S. Economy: Safety and Privacy," Statement Before the Senate Committee on Commerce, Science, and Transportation, January 15, 2014. www.aclu.org.

CBS Local   "Drone Scare for LAX-Bound Flight Reignites Safety Debate," February 9, 2015. http://losangeles.cbslocal.com.

Paul Cochrane   "Peaceful Drones," *MIT Technology Review*, March 26, 2015.

David Cortright   "How Drones Are Changing Warfare: License to Kill," *Cato Unbound*, January 9, 2012. www.cato-unbound.org.

David Cortright   "The Scary Prospect of Global Drone Warfare," CNN, October 19, 2011. www.cnn.com.

Catherine Crump and Jay Stanley   "Why Americans Are Saying No to Domestic Drones," *Slate*, February 11, 2013. www.slate.com.

Jeremy Diamond   "US Drone Strike Accidentally Killed Two Hostages," CNN, April 23, 2015. www.cnn.com.

Laura Donnelly   "Drones Could Be Used to Seek out Arteries to Prevent Heart Attacks," *Telegraph* (UK), February 8, 2015.

Kimberlu Dozier   "Human Rights Groups Criticize US Drone Program," *Huffington Post*, October 22, 2013. www.huffingtonpost.com.

Dronelife News   "How Sexy Headlines May Be
                      Shaping the Drone Debate," July 30,
                      2014. http://dronelife.com.

Bill Gertz   "China Preparing for Drone Warfare:
                      PLA Plans to Build 42,000 UAVs,
                      Pentagon Says," *Washington Free
                      Beacon*, May 8, 2015.

Ben Gielow   "AUVSI Tells Congress—Pace of UAS
                      Integration Unacceptable,"
                      Association for Unmanned Vehicle
                      Systems International, March 11,
                      2014. www.auvsi.org.

Andrew Griffin   "TGI Friday Drone Crashes into
                      Woman's Face and Cuts It Open in
                      Restaurant," *Independent* (UK),
                      December 9, 2014.

Neema Singh   "Unchecked Government Drones?
Guliani   Not Over My Backyard," *The Hill*,
                      March 24, 2015. http://thehill.com.

Gregory Hall   "Drones' Promise Weighed Against
                      Privacy, Safety," *Courier Journal*,
                      December 14, 2014.

Elizabeth   "Audit: DHS Drone Program
Harrington   Ineffective at Border Security,"
                      Washington Free Beacon, January 6,
                      2015.

Julian Hattem   "Drones Crash onto White House
                      Agenda," *The Hill*, January 29, 2015.
                      http://thehill.com.

W.J. Hennigan   "City in Virginia Passes Anti-Drone
                         Resolution," *Los Angeles Times*,
                         February 6, 2013.

Andres Jauregui   "'Drone Boning' Is Why You Can't
                         Have Sex in Public," *Huffington Post*,
                         December 22, 2014.
                         www.huffingtonpost.com.

Leo King   "Mind-Controlled Drone Scientists
                         Work on Groundbreaking Flight,"
                         Forbes, February 25, 2015.

David LaGesse   "If Drones Make You Nervous, Think
                         of Them as Flying Donkeys,"
                         National Public Radio, March 31,
                         2015. www.npr.org.

Josh Lederman   "Secret Service to Conduct Drone
                         Exercises Over Washington,"
                         Associated Press, February 24, 2015.
                         http://hosted.ap.org.

Tammy Leitner   "How a Drone Could Spoof Wi-Fi,
and Lisa   Steal Your Data," NBC Chicago, May
Capitanini   5, 2015. www.nbcchicago.com.

Barry Levine   "Drones Overhead in LA's Valley Are
                         Tracking Mobile Devices' Locations,"
                         Venture Beat, February 23, 2015.
                         http://venturebeat.com.

Daniel Lippman   "Drones Fly into the Political Ad
                         Wars," *Politico*, February 7, 2015.
                         www.politico.com.

Ryan Lovelace   "Drones in Our Future: On Our
                    Border with Mexico, Both Drug
                    Smugglers and the CBP Use Them,"
                    National Review, February 4, 2015.

Joan Lowy   "Battlefield Stigma Complicates
                    Peaceful Drone Use at Home,"
                    Gazettenet.com, March 30, 2013.
                    www.gazettenet.com.

Joan Lowy   "Proposed Rules for Drones Envision
                    Routine Commercial Use," Associated
                    Press, February 15, 2015.
                    http://apnews.myway.com.

Michael B. Marois   "Creeps Embrace a New Tool:
                    Peeping Drones," Bloomberg
                    Business, May 5, 2015.
                    www.bloomberg.com.

William Marra   "Understanding 'The Loop': Humans
and Sonia McNeil   and the Next Drone Generations,"
                    Issues in Governance Studies, August
                    2012. www.brookings.edu.

Gary Martin and   "Drone Makers Push Congress to
Viveca Novak   Open Skies to Surveillance," *Houston
                    Chronicle*, November 24, 2012.

Mark Mazzetti   "Deep Support in Washington for
and Matt Apuzzo   CIA's Drone Missions," *New York
                    Times*, April 25, 2015.

Kalaya'an   "This Is How You Fight Drones,"
Mendoza   *Human Rights Now*, November 14,
                    2013. http://blog.amnestyusa.org.

Asher Moses — "Flying Drones a Safety Threat at Airports," *Sydney Morning Herald*, September 11, 2012.

Greg Nichols — "Swarm Robots Poised to Fly Amid Acquisitions and Military Investment," *Robotics/ZD Net*, April 14, 2015. www.zdnet.com.

Mickey Osterreicher and Alicia Calzada — "Have Drone, Will Gather News," *News Photographer*, January/February 2015.

Ed Pilkington — "Amazon Tests Delivery Drones at Secret Canada Site After US Frustration in British Columbia," *Guardian* (UK), March 30, 2015.

Avery Plaw — "Drone Strikes Save Lives, American and Other," *New York Times*, November 14, 2012.

Mark Prado — "Golden Gate Bridge Officials Want to Keep Drones Away from Span," *Marin Independent Journal*, April 24, 2015.

PRNewswire-USNewswire — "Drones Reduce Number of American Troops, Former Clinton White House Spokesman Robert Weiner and Defense Analyst Tom Sherman Say Liberals and Conservatives Should Both Advocate Them," October 10, 2014. www.prnewswire.com.

ProCon.org — "Drones—Pros and Cons," August 11, 2014. http://drones.procon.org.

Brad Reed   "The World's Tiniest Drone Shows Privacy May Be Dead for Good," BGR, March 5, 2015. http://bgr.com.

Reuters   "Mini Army Drones Developed," March 10, 2015. www.reuters.com.

Barrie Rokeach "As a Pilot, I'm Not Keen on Sharing the Skies with Drones," *San Francisco Chronicle*, May 13, 2015.

Alice Ross   "Is Congressional Oversight Tough Enough on Drones?," Bureau of Investigative Journalism, August 1, 2013. www.thebureauinvestigates.com.

Luke Runyon "As Rules Get Sorted Out, Drones May Transform Agriculture Industry," National Public Radio, February 16, 2015. www.npr.org.

William Saletan "In Defense of Drones: They're the Worst Form of War, Except for All the Others," *Slate*, February 19, 2013. www.slate.com.

Henry Samuel "Drone Spotted Near Charlie Hebdo as Ten More Fly Over Paris," *Telegraph* (UK), March 4, 2015.

Monica Sarkar "Security from the Sky: Indian City to Use Pepper-Spray Drones for Crowd Control," CNN, April 9, 2015. www.cnn.com.

Michael Schmidt "Drones Smuggle Contraband Over Prison Walls," *New York Times*, April 22, 2015.

Connor Adams   "Commercial Drones' Rise Seen as
Sheets   Growing Danger to Traditional
                      Aircraft," *International Business
                      Times*, April 25, 2014.

Aaron Smith   "US Views of Technology and the
                      Future—Science in the Next Fifty
                      Years," Pew Research Center, April 17,
                      2014. www.pewinternet.org.

Andrew Stobo   "Drones for Human Rights," *New
Sniderman and   York Times*, January 30, 2012.
Mark Hanis

Jay Stanley and   "Protecting Privacy from Aerial
Catherine Crump   Surveillance: Recommendations for
                      Government Use of Drone Aircraft,"
                      ACLU, 2011. www.aclu.org.

Amie Stepanovich   "The Future of Drones in America:
                      Law Enforcement and Privacy
                      Considerations—Hearing Before the
                      Committee of the Judiciary United
                      States Senate," US Government
                      Printing Office, March 20, 2013.
                      www.gpo.gov.

Laura Sydell   "As Drones Fly in Cities and Yards,
                      So Do the Complaints," National
                      Public Radio, May 12, 2014.
                      www.npr.org.

Daniel Terdiman   "Flying Lampshades: Cirque du Soleil
                      Plays with Drones," CNET,
                      September 23, 2014. www.cnet.com.

Patrick Tucker   "The Nine Strangest Flying Robots
                    from the World's Biggest Drone
                    Show," *Defense One*, May 8, 2015.
                    www.defenseone.com.

Muhsin Usman   "How America Is Fueling
                    Radicalization of Muslims and How
                    to Reverse It," *Huffington Post*, July 6,
                    2012. www.huffingtonpost.com.

Steve Watson   "Security, Privacy Experts Testify to
                    Congress on Spy Drones," *Prison
                    Planet*, July 19, 2012.
                    www.prisonplanet.com.

John Watts   "Drone, Baby, Drone . . . If You Want
                    More Terrorists," Campaign for
                    Liberty, February 27, 2013.
                    www.campaignforliberty.org.

John Whitehead   "The Micro-Drone Revolution:
                    Roachbots, Ravens, Mosquitos, and
                    More," CNS News, April 15, 2013.
                    http://cnsnews.com.

Craig Whitlock   "FAA Proposes Rules for Drone Use;
                    Obama Issues Curbs on
                    Surveillance," *Washington Post*,
                    February 15, 2015.

Craig Whitlock   "How Crashing Drones Are Exposing
                    Secrets About US War Operations,"
                    Washington Post, March 25, 2015.

Ben Wolfgang   "Drone Privacy Scare," *Washington
                    Times*, February 15, 2012.

Index